THE NEW **COLLEGE** REALITY

THE NEW COLLEGE REALITY

Make College Work for Your Career

Bonnie Kerrigan Snyder, DEd, CCPS

Avon, Massachusetts

Published by
Adams Media, a division of F+W Media, Inc.
57 Littlefield Street, Avon, MA 02322. U.S.A.
www.adamsmedia.com

ISBN 10: 1-4405-3012-2
ISBN 13: 978-1-4405-3012-8
eISBN 10: 1-4405-3332-6
eISBN 13: 978-1-4405-3332-7

Printed in the United States of America.

10 9 8 7 6 5 4 3 2 1

Library of Congress Cataloging-in-Publication Data
is available from the publisher.

This publication is designed to provide accurate and authoritative information with regard to the subject matter covered. It is sold with the understanding that the publisher is not engaged in rendering legal, accounting, or other professional advice. If legal advice or other expert assistance is required, the services of a competent professional person should be sought.

—From a *Declaration of Principles* jointly adopted by a Committee of the American Bar Association and a Committee of Publishers and Associations

Many of the designations used by manufacturers and sellers to distinguish their product are claimed as trademarks. Where those designations appear in this book and Adams Media was aware of a trademark claim, the designations have been printed with initial capital letters.

This book is available at quantity discounts for bulk purchases.
For information, please call 1-800-289-0963.

DEDICATION

This book is dedicated to college-bound high school students and their parents

ACKNOWLEDGMENTS

This book would never have been written without the motivation provided by my daughters. The terror of paying for their higher education was all the inspiration I needed to launch this writing project. To borrow from the great pianist Victor Borge, "I wish to thank my parents for making it all possible, and I wish to thank my children for making it necessary."

I would like to thank Beth Abate Bacon for reading the earliest drafts and for providing excellent feedback and much-needed encouragement to continue. It meant a lot at a time when I easily could have abandoned this time-consuming effort. Thanks also to Colleen Jacobsen for attending my earliest speaking events and listening to and supporting the development of this idea.

I couldn't possibly have found a better agent than Miriam Altshuler, whose representation has been superb. She has been an ongoing pleasure to work with and stuck with me even when it looked like this book might never see the light of day. Beyond being an enthusiastic supporter and reliable source of excellent advice, she has also been an enjoyable companion on the college parent's journey.

I am deeply appreciative of the keen insights of my editor, Peter Archer, and everyone at Adams Media in improving my manuscript. They are great at what they do, and I couldn't have asked for a more talented team.

I am indebted to all the insightful writers who have previously addressed this important topic. Each view has expanded my understanding of the subject and I hope that they appreciate my contribution to this ongoing conversation. I also wish to extend my gratitude to unemployed college friends who generously shared their stories with me.

Thanks, especially, to Mark for tolerating and supporting my ongoing writing addiction.

CONTENTS

YESTERDAY'S ADVICE IS NOT GOOD ENOUGH ANYMORE

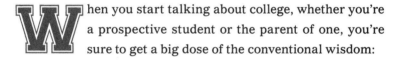

When you start talking about college, whether you're a prospective student or the parent of one, you're sure to get a big dose of the conventional wisdom:

- A college degree will set you apart

- College will guarantee a good job

- Save money for college

- A college degree is always a good investment

- Student loans are "good debt" because you will easily be able to repay them with the higher earnings you can expect to receive as a college graduate

Most people accept and act on this advice without questioning or examining it, because it is so ingrained in our thinking. They consider these assertions self-evident.

These maxims still sound good, but as my own children approached college age, I began to suspect that many of these comfortable, timeworn statements just didn't apply anymore. For example, my friends and acquaintances might say that college is the route to a better life, but I knew many recent graduates who were stuck in low-paying jobs that don't require a college degree.

I watched as the children of friends and neighbors finished their degrees. Large numbers of them moved back home and took jobs in landscaping, retail, and food service. They could have acquired these jobs straight out of high school, but now they had to use a big part of their meager wages to pay back their hefty student loans. I also knew many college graduates, of all ages, who were unemployed—some of them for a year or longer. It became obvious to me that a college degree alone was no longer the sure ticket to the so-called "good life"—a middle-class job with benefits—that it was a generation or two ago.

I thought back to my own college-to-employment experience. I grew up in a family that emphasized the importance of education, and the old ways of thinking about college had a big effect on me. I worked hard in school and matriculated as an undergraduate at Harvard. For the next four years I kept my head in a book and didn't pay much attention to the job market or economy. I trusted that my degree would take care of my employment prospects. Then I graduated into the recession that coincided with the stock market crash of 1987. To say this was a big wake-up call would be a dramatic understatement.

THE REALITY OF POST-GRADUATION LIFE

I had assumed that if I graduated from an Ivy League institution, employers would be banging on my door, desperate to hire me. Through a misty haze I saw myself choosing between competing offers, effortlessly easing into a comfortable lifetime career.

It didn't quite turn out that way. During my initial job search I did a great deal of pavement pounding and found myself in several temp agencies. I quickly discovered that the world wasn't beating a path to my door, even with my freshly minted English degree. Becoming self-supporting was going to be harder than I had anticipated. My first offer was for an editorial assistant position with a publisher in New York City at $13,000 a year—a bad salary even in the late 1980s. Apparently, a college degree alone, even from an elite institution, was no guarantee of a high-paying job.

Flash forward to today. New college graduates face an even less welcoming job market. They hold record-breaking amounts of debt acquired in pursuit of degrees that may never give them the high salaries they anticipated. Instead of temp work, they are being offered unpaid internships. In the wake of the Great Recession of 2008–2009, the fierce competition for jobs shows no signs of abating any time soon.

It's a rare parent these days who does not feel anxious about her child's future prospects. The reality is that there are good reasons to worry. As I write, one in five Americans is unemployed or underemployed. Think college graduates are immune? Think again. Just 20 percent of graduating students who applied for jobs have one, according to the National Association of Colleges and Employers. This is down from 51 percent in 2007.

Furthermore, these unemployed graduates do not show up in official unemployment numbers because in order to be counted as "unemployed," you first have to have a job.

No longer can we sit back and safely assume that every college graduate is going to be well positioned to earn a salary sufficient to maintain a middle-class lifestyle—or even to put food on the table, let alone pay back student loans. Higher education and the employment marketplace have changed so dramatically over the past generation that the old rules about college need a complete makeover to remain relevant. We need to consider what advice will help this generation of young adults to find success in the world as it is now.

Families have to take a fresh look at the college value proposition to confront these changed present-day realities:

- **A college degree now costs more than ever, will not guarantee a job, and can be a risky investment, if you approach it imprudently.**

- **The financial returns on a Bachelor's degree are down, and higher education offers a much less reliable path to upward mobility for today's college students.**

- **Today's young adults are facing one of the most overheated college markets ever, while simultaneously confronting some of the worst employment prospects in American history.**

In short, families today need help, and outmoded advice can actually do more harm than good.

I hope that this book will inspire you to look at college in a new way. At the end of the college road, when the tuition bills finally stop coming, my fondest wish is that new graduates will be prepared to enter the workforce smoothly as independent adults. Further, I hope they'll be able to do this without the burden of student debt crushing their future dreams and aspirations. College, after all, is a means of getting where you want to go in life; it is not the destination.

Likewise, college is a time for parents to begin making preparations for their own retirement dreams after the kids finally leave the nest—a milestone that will be difficult to achieve if the entire nest egg is spent on excessive college bills or if graduates are unable to support themselves. It's time to do some updating of our cherished assumptions to match the reality that the next generation will confront. We cannot succeed today by looking backward and offering stale, worn-out advice; instead, we must change our way of thinking to match what will be required of us in the coming hard years.

—Bonnie Kerrigan Snyder, DEd
August 2011

THE MOST COVETED STATUS SYMBOL OF ALL

The selective process of college admissions has always generated a lot of anxiety and pressure. High school students—I know quite a few of them—can become obsessed with trying to craft the perfect combination of transcripts, references, essays, and extracurricular activities to excite the admissions committee and move their applications to the coveted Admit pile.

Getting into the "right" college used to be the ultimate status symbol. You could cruise the neighborhood with your Yale, Harvard, or other Ivy League decal on your car window, and heads would turn. A prestigious admissions offer signaled elite status, bragging rights, and presumably ready entry to the most desirable careers.

These days, there is a prize even more highly coveted than the admissions offer: the first job offer. Unfortunately, for an increasing number of college graduates, including those from highly selective colleges, it is more elusive than ever. Today, the competition is gruelingly intense, both for admission to upper-tier schools and for decent paying jobs afterward.

Then, there's the growing struggle to pay for the degree. Many middle-class families, including quite possibly yours, are in a state of financial panic over spiraling tuition costs. More than one parent confessed to me that she lay awake at night, gripping the blankets, with the thought of paying for college swirling around and around in her mind. It's no wonder. College costs have risen far faster than the general inflation rate for a long time. The price to attend an elite private university for four years now approaches a staggering quarter of $1 million.

═══COLLEGE BY THE NUMBERS═══

In 1988, the share of a median household's income devoted to higher education was 22 percent; in 2011, it was more than 50 percent. According to a recent report by the College Board, if wages increased at the same rate as tuition, the average American family would be earning $77,000 a year, but in reality, the median income is just $33,000.

═══════════════════════$═══════════════════════

We are at a financial tipping point. Most middle-class students and their families see no way to meet growing tuition costs other than to assume student loan debt. For many of them, these debt loads will prove crushing and unsustainable, as the rising default and postponement rates indicate.

The most painful blow of all, however, is that after all of the hard work and financial sacrifice that goes into earning a college degree the student may face unemployment. Even for those who do find jobs, many are discovering that they cannot command salaries high enough to justify the cost of earning the degree.

FOCUS ON THE JOB

To make the college investment pay off, *students must become more proactive about focusing their educational opportunities on the ultimate goal of landing a job.* An effective college education today begins and ends with deliberate career planning. College is a time to cultivate a network of career contacts while building a resume of documented work experience and enthusiastic professional references. In short, students must go beyond what their classmates are doing, and what their professors are demanding, to ensure that they will have what it takes to find employment and support themselves no matter what the economic conditions are like when they graduate.

The conventional college wisdom, the wise sayings that your friends and family poured into your ears, is clearly failing many of today's students. *The New College Reality* provides new strategies for avoiding the most expensive higher education mistakes and launching graduates successfully into independent, employed adulthoods.

Throughout this book, I'll present both the old rules that used to apply to picking a college, constructing a course of study, and finding a job and the new rules that are essential for financial survival in today's world. Here are the rules:

1

OLD RULE: A college degree will set you apart.

NEW RULE: *College is the new high school diploma. Supplement it.*

2

OLD RULE: Go to college to decide what you would like to major in.

NEW RULE: *Focus on a career and major before choosing the college.*

3

OLD RULE: Focus on your GPA in college to ensure you get hired.

NEW RULE: *Focus on the job market to ensure you get hired.*

4

OLD RULE: Begin college visits in the Admissions Office.

NEW RULE: *Begin college visits in the career center.*

5

OLD RULE: You will "feel" which college is right when you visit.

NEW RULE: *Choose a college with your head, not your heart.*

6

OLD RULE: Count on your adviser to map out a course schedule and plan of study.

NEW RULE: *Double-check everything a college adviser tells you.*

7

OLD RULE: It doesn't matter what you major in, as long as you get your degree.

NEW RULE: *Majors matter.*

8 **OLD RULE:** A college degree ensures financial security.

NEW RULE: *College can be a risky financial investment; hedge your bets.*

9 **OLD RULE:** Go to the best school that you can get into.

NEW RULE: *Go where the deal is best.*

10 **OLD RULE:** A college degree is always a good investment at any price.

NEW RULE: *Never pay the asking price; hold out for a better deal.*

11 **OLD RULE:** Financial aid levels the economic playing field.

NEW RULE: *Financial aid makes college more unaffordable. Learn the system.*

12 **OLD RULE:** Rely on the financial aid office to help you figure out how to pay for college.

NEW RULE: *Financial aid officers work for the college. Do your own research.*

13 **OLD RULE:** Financial aid is distributed equitably.

NEW RULE: *Be first in line for aid, because it is first come, first served.*

14 **OLD RULE:** Student loans are "good debt."

NEW RULE: *Base your college borrowing on your expected entry-level earnings.*

15

OLD RULE: Save money for college.

NEW RULE: *Savers are penalized by the financial aid system. Shelter money instead.*

16

OLD RULE: There is nothing you can do about high tuition.

NEW RULE: *Everything is negotiable, from tuition to how long it takes to graduate.*

17

OLD RULE: Liberal arts graduates can do "anything."

NEW RULE: *Make sure your degree has a clear relation to existing or emerging jobs.*

18

OLD RULE: The name of your undergraduate college is very important.

NEW RULE: *Your last degree is what matters most.*

19

OLD RULE: A college degree is necessary for a middle-class lifestyle.

NEW RULE: *A profession or skill in demand is necessary for a middle-class lifestyle.*

20

OLD RULE: Your college degree will get you a job.

NEW RULE: *Your resume, "brand," and personal contacts will get you a job.*

21

OLD RULE: Once the kid graduates, he's on his own financially.

NEW RULE: *Parents may have to help graduates more now after college, especially with their first job search.*

22

OLD RULE: Find a safe, secure job and stay in it until retirement.

NEW RULE: *Always be prepared to make your own job.*

PART I

MAKING COLLEGE WORK FOR YOU TODAY

Mundus novus

CHAPTER 1

WHAT'S A COLLEGE DEGREE WORTH THESE DAYS?

My daughter and I sat in our kitchen and looked at one another. In front of us on the table were spread out a swath of pamphlets, letters, folders, and printouts. My laptop was open and quietly humming, showing on its screen a maze of spreadsheets. I rubbed my forehead and blinked to clear my eyes. It felt as if I'd been staring at the computer screen forever.

Together, we were grappling with one of the biggest decisions we, as a family, would ever make. Where was my daughter going to go to college?

This scene may seem familiar to you. Already, you may be in the midst of these discussions. You've probably talked about the value of a college education, whether you're a parent or a child. Perhaps, if you're a student you want to be well educated. You're excited by the thought of reading great literature, meeting interesting people, and engaging in stimulating discussions with enthusiastic classmates and knowledgeable professors. Or you may be dreaming of the whole college experience—making friends, experiencing independence, and at the same time absorbing new thoughts and information. If you're a parent, you want the best for your child, to give her or him the most thorough and valuable education available.

There's one reason for attending college, however, that probably tops the rest: both of you believe that it will improve the student's earning power and increase her chances of having a better career. Americans generally expect that college attendance will pay off in the workforce, because traditionally that's just what it's done.

WHAT ARE THE REAL FINANCIAL BENEFITS?

For years, the media and politicians shouted from the rooftops that a college graduate can expect to earn $1 million more than a high school graduate over the course of a career. Backed by this comfortable assertion, generations of families and students willingly assumed student loans to finance the degree. With that extra $1 million, they thought, repaying the loans would be a snap!

Or would it? Today, many economists are reevaluating this $1 million figure. They now estimate that the expected earnings for a college graduate are actually probably closer to half that amount. For example, an economist for The College Board found that the average college graduate could expect to earn about $800,000 more than a high school graduate.

Still pretty good though, right? Yes, until you consider that the degree must be financed with current dollars and the future earnings will be subject to inflation. When you take that into account, the value of the difference in today's dollars would be worth closer to $450,000. Of course, this does not consider the cost of the degree itself, which is now approaching $240,000 at the most expensive schools. Subtract that out and the real net value of a degree, in current dollars, is closer to $300,000.

The bottom line is that the costs keep rising while the rate of increase in the value of the degree is slowing. Supply and demand has a lot to do with this. Today, a majority of high school students expect to go to college. As the number of degree holders in the general population grows, the payoff for each college degree presumably declines. The result, you won't be surprised to hear, is that many college graduates are having more difficulty finding college-level employment worthy of the time and expense they incurred securing the diploma.

And, while you're at it, don't forget to consider the cost of interest on debt, which will significantly inflate the costs if you take loans to finance college. Few people realize that the biggest lifetime cost of paying for college for many students will not be tuition, room, board, or textbooks. It will be loan interest.

A College Bubble?

There's another important factor to consider in making smart decisions about college in a shifting economy. The current college climate has all the earmarks of a classic economic bubble.

- **Spiraling costs, which bear no relationship to what consumers can afford and are disconnecting from actual returns on the investment.**

- Euphoric demand, with a ready list of consumers lining up and actually *competing* to purchase the product.

- Intense belief in the product, which sometimes seems to defy reason or stubborn facts.

- Ready access to easily obtained credit helping consumers to finance the purchase, even when it is clearly beyond their means—the only thing propping up this economic house of cards.

═══COLLEGE BY THE NUMBERS═══

Instapundit blogger Glenn Reynolds tells of a discussion he had with accountant friends who told him that their degrees had cost them between $3,000– $4,000 per year in the 1980s, for a total of around $16,000. Their starting salaries were $17,000. Today, an accounting degree at the same school costs $168,000 while a starting accountant earns about $45,000. Reynolds asserts that many other college degrees have seen a similar decline in their payoff because the return has roughly kept pace with inflation, while the required investment has run far, far ahead. This changes all the value calculations.

═══════════════════$═══════════════════

Let's see . . . we have spiraling costs, irrational demand, and easy credit fueling the increase in prices. That's the classic definition of a market bubble, all right. Demand for college degrees continues to grow, even in light of demonstrated evidence that there is not sufficient demand for existing college graduates in the workforce.

If you think this sounds similar to the 2008 housing bubble that left an astonishing number of American families owing more on their overpriced homes than they are worth, you're right. Too many families and students are overleveraging their college educations to the point that they find themselves underwater on expensive loans for a bachelor's degree with little economic value.

During the housing bubble, one of the first signs of trouble was the fact that home prices rose much higher than comparable rents. In other words, if you bought a house at market value, you couldn't find renters to pay the cost of covering the monthly financing on it. The carrying costs were higher than the income the property produced. Likewise, one sign of a developing college tuition bubble is that graduates aren't finding jobs that pay enough to cover the financing required to obtain the degrees. Then, just as with the housing bubble, they default. This is already occurring: The number of student loan defaults is mushrooming at record rates.

YOU NEED TO STEP BACK

There's only one sane response to this overheated college market: We've got to exercise the kind of purchasing restraint that was so sorely needed during the height of the housing bubble. Think of it this way: If you needed a home during 2006, you would have been much better off renting than buying one with an inflated price, even though that might not have been your first choice. Likewise, a student pursuing a college education today needs to seek out affordable postsecondary alternatives and cut costs whenever possible in order to increase the likelihood that the returns on the degree will be positive.

As a family, you must exercise financial caution and consider doing the *opposite* of what the majority of other higher education consumers are doing. Following the crowd in a market bubble is a sure way to wind up in trouble when it pops.

So let's assume that we are in a higher education bubble and behave accordingly. You must look at every aspect of the college experience with fresh eyes and reconsider your existing assumptions about postsecondary education.

R E A L I T Y   R U L E   # 1

OLD RULE:	NEW RULE:
A college degree will set you apart.	*College is the new high school diploma. Supplement it.*

Once upon a time, merely having a bachelor's degree—in any field—was enough to set you apart in the job market. Very few people possessed them, and so having the credential signaled (rightly or wrongly) higher-than-average intelligence and accomplishment to potential employers. It got you hired and virtually guaranteed you a pretty nice job.

Those days are long gone, for a number of reasons.

Increase in Graduates

First, consider how dramatically the number of college graduates has increased in America over the past fifty or so years. Attending college is practically an assumed rite of passage. Of course, this increased demand for higher education is one of the factors driving and sustaining today's tuition rates. One of the main reasons that many colleges today charge such high prices is simply because they can.

Based on current dropout rates, about half of today's college students will ultimately fail to earn a degree, but that still means that in the near future college graduates will comprise about 35 percent of the population. At this rate, it is easy to imagine a future in which half of the American population is college-educated. It's also hard to see how a bachelor's degree will continue to confer much extra status.

Believe it or not, high school diplomas were once valued as highly as college diplomas are today. Back in 1900, a high school diploma was sufficient to secure a graduate a comfortable middle-class existence and a salary level sufficient to purchase a house and support a family. At the beginning of the twentieth century, the number of high school graduates was the same as the number of college graduates in 1950: only 6 percent. Those early high school graduates could expect roughly the same employment preferences that college graduates could expect at mid-century. In 1940, 25 percent of people had at least a high school diploma. By 1998, 83 percent of adults had at least a high school diploma, and employers were no longer impressed.

A college degree has become the new high school diploma—the bare minimal credential for entry into the workforce. When millions of college graduates are working in jobs that don't require college degrees, you can see from the statistics I just cited that a college diploma no longer guarantees a graduate employment at the college level. The competition for jobs has risen right along with the number of awarded baccalaureate degrees. One college expert described the college diploma as a hunter's license rather than any sort of guarantee of employment.

══COLLEGE BY THE NUMBERS══

In 1950, only 6.2 percent of the American population possessed a college degree. College attendance rates began to climb during the 1960s and really took off when the baby boomer generation reached college age. By 1980, 16.2 percent of Americans had a college degree. Today, that number stands close to 30 percent. A century ago only about 2 percent of American adults graduated from college whereas today, nearly 71 percent of all high school students attempt college. This is a staggering change; all but 30 percent now plan to pursue higher education.

═══════════════**$**═══════════════

A college education still obviously has inherent worth, but a college diploma's value in the workforce has declined while the price of obtaining one soars. *In terms of employment power in the marketplace, the college degree is now roughly equivalent to what a high school diploma once was.* College alone is not going to guarantee all graduates high-paying jobs, anymore, yet most high school students still plan to attend. What, then, can we do to improve the odds for enrollees, in light of these unsettling facts?

THINK "COLLEGE-*PLUS*"

The main way to deal with credential inflation is to add something extra to your college degree. I call it College-*Plus* because students need to add something valuable and specific to the basic bachelor's degree to stand out from other job applicants.

Emphasizing Competition

One way many students try to accomplish this is by seeking admission to the most competitive colleges. You might naturally assume that employers will look more favorably upon you if you've graduated from a selective school. This sounds like one obvious way to add something extra to your degree.

It's true that certain elite companies only recruit at a limited number of top schools, so if you really want to work at one of these major corporations, this is a good option to pursue. However, the admissions frenzy this creates at top schools contributes to rising tuition costs, and you have to wonder whether or not the payback for attending an elite undergraduate institution is worth the higher prices they normally command. The numbers game also means that there is a limit to the number of students who can be admitted to the few top schools. Because of this, you should consider other ways to make a standard college degree stand out.

Stronger Credentials

Another way of attracting attention in the labor market is to supplement the bachelor's degree with other convincing credentials. For you, this could mean attending graduate or professional school after college. If bachelor's degrees are the new high school diplomas, then presumably master and doctoral degrees are the new bachelor and master's degrees. In fact, growing numbers of college graduates are pursuing this option. Graduate school is an expensive and time-consuming avenue to pursue, though, so you should consider it in light of your abilities, stamina, and aspirations. For parents who are assisting with the costs, graduate school also increases overall higher education fees, which merely underscores the need to reduce expenditures at the undergraduate level for most families.

Specialized Career Training

What if graduate school is not the right option? In that case, a smart strategy might be to consider pursuing additional credentials that provide access to restricted opportunities in the job market. You can acquire some of these professional credentials through traditional college programs, such as teaching certificates or the preparation necessary to sit for licensure exams in fields such as nursing or accounting. Only accredited applicants are qualified to work in these fields, so this reduces the employment competition.

There are also accrediting organizations in numerous other specific fields that can provide certifications that will help you stand out from the crowd. These are less well known. To find a comprehensive list of these sorts of opportunities, take a look at the Credentials Center on *www.careeronestop.org/credentialing/ credentialinghome.asp.*

Many of these credentialing programs are not only skills-building opportunities but also valuable networking avenues. For example, there are certificates for Quality Technicians, Mechanical Drafters, Computer Hacking Investigators, and Energy Auditors, to name a few. If you're a recent college graduate, don't turn your nose up at these practical opportunities. They look great on resumes and specific training and certification *plus* a college degree is a very powerful combination.

The people and connections you can meet through these training opportunities can open doors and provide important insights into trends in specific career fields and existing or upcoming job opportunities. They can provide ready access to working, adult professionals who know an industry inside and out.

BEYOND THE BACHELOR'S

Many college graduates may balk at the idea that the bachelor's degree is not enough, anymore. This is an understandable mindset, given the long hard slog from kindergarten through commencement. It was enough for your parents, so why not you? After all the time and money spent on college, it is not surprising if students feel they cannot afford to pursue any more credentials. However, this type of thinking merely limits the competition for those willing to think creatively and move beyond the bachelor's.

Aside from adding additional credentials, you can distinguish yourself by gaining valuable work experience and garnering excellent employer references along the way. Look closely at colleges that emphasize real-world experience and high quality internship placements as part of their educational programming.

Employers like to hire people with experience and are often unwilling to take a risk on someone with no work history.

Back when I was a teenager, it seemed like we all had jobs. It was very unusual for a high school kid not to work during summer vacation. We scooped ice cream, waited tables, and worked amusements at the boardwalk. We scoffed at our silly jobs back then, but we needed the money and would have felt left out if we weren't working. It was what everyone was doing.

Today, it seems as though a working adolescent is the exception rather than the rule. The good news is that this means that having work experience on your resume is a great way to stand out in front of potential employers. Fortunately, some of the best jobs are available right on campus. Upper-level students can sometimes find professional-caliber work in laboratories, offices, and in their academic field of interest, which can lead to great letters of recommendation. The one catch is that many of the best jobs are only available to those who qualify for federal work-study programs, which helps to cover some of the wages.

Federal work-study opportunities are an important reason why families must do everything possible to qualify for federal aid, as I'll discuss in Part II. Students who do not qualify for aid typically also do not qualify to work on campus and will have to seek off-campus jobs, often in low-skill fields that will not enhance their resumes much.

A surprising number of students who qualify for work-study refuse to take these subsidized campus work opportunities, preferring instead to enjoy their free time or leverage the future with more loans. This is a big mistake. If you qualify for work-study, take full advantage of the opportunities available on campus before looking elsewhere for employment. Incidentally, one of the best jobs to get on campus is in the career center, which provides access to all the latest job and internship postings—a huge advantage for any undergraduate.

Now we'll turn to the practical realities of gaining admission to colleges today. As with everything else about the educational scene, much has changed.

═══COLLEGE BY THE NUMBERS═══

The sad reality is that employment rates for young people have been declining for several years, making it harder for them to prove themselves. It's much more difficult for a young person to find a job today, which in my view is a terrible shame. The current youth (ages 16–24) unemployment rate is 19.1 percent—the highest on record since data collection began in 1948, according to the Bureau of Labor Statistics.

═══════════════$═══════════════

CHAPTER 2

PLANNING FOR LIFE BEYOND COLLEGE

REALITY RULE #2

OLD RULE:	NEW RULE:
Go to college to decide what you would like to major in.	*Focus on a career and major before choosing the college.*

ollege planning is tremendously exciting. When you and your parents sit down to talk about it, there are so many decisions to be made:

- Do you want to go to college near home or far away?

- Would you prefer a big or small campus?

- Are any of your friends going there?

- What are the dorms like?

- What about the dining hall?

Then, there's the really big question: Will you get in?

These are all valid concerns. However, they overlook the most important one of all: *What are you going to college for?* When it's all said and done, where is college going to take you? Higher education will prove most valuable when students think *beyond* college to their ultimate career aspirations. This mindset helps students make the most of their college opportunities.

Years ago, my parents (and others) used to ask me all the time, What do you want to be when you grow up? I wasn't the only one; others were asking my friends the same question. Well-meaning relatives would corner their young grandchildren or nephews and nieces and pose that stumper.

Somehow, over the years, parents and others seem to have gotten away from asking kids that uncomfortable question. Maybe they're afraid of pigeonholing youngsters at an early age. Maybe, as parents, we remember squirming when older relatives asked the same thing of us, so we refrain from putting our children in that position. It seems we all want to keep our options open as long as possible, and we are extending this courtesy to the next generation. While this may be fine during times of unlimited opportunity, this is a luxury fewer of us can afford.

Now that college can cost more than a house, it's time to start asking that important question again. Career planning is probably the most overlooked part of the college preparation process for most students. Instead, it needs to be a fundamental part. This is especially true if—like most of us—you're a family of average or modest means. Unless you're rich, you must approach college and your subsequent career with greater purpose and economy of action.

CAREER PLANNING WITH A HIGH SCHOOL STUDENT

Unfortunately, most American high schools don't do a very good job of helping students with careers. What they do best is prepare students for college. High school teachers and counselors all attended college, so this is an area they understand well. Beyond that, everything becomes rather blurry, which is a big part of the reason why adolescents are often confused about career direction. According to Kenneth Gray and Edwin Herr, authors of the book *Other Ways to Win,*

> *"Relatively few teens have taken the time to think about their career plans, even though getting a good job is why they enroll in college. Most have this faith—perhaps hope is a more appropriate term—that there will be ample commensurate employment for 4-year college graduates. Thus all they have to do is get a degree in just about any field, and a high paying professional job is guaranteed."*

Unfortunately, as Gray and Herr explain, students' optimism is largely unfounded. The authors indicate that each year there will be only about half as many college-level jobs for graduates as are needed. Consequently, nearly half of all college graduates wind up underemployed, in jobs that do not require a college degree. That's a frightening number: Fully 50 percent of students might as well not have gone to college for all the impact their degree has on their job!

Career confusion and indecision last well into college for many students, who may avoid declaring a major as long as possible. The developmental psychologist James Marcia refers to this period of delay before making a career commitment as a "moratorium." The problem is that this moratorium stage seems to be lasting longer and longer while college grows ever more costly.

A student such as my daughter might want to spend the first two years of a college program deciding what she would like to major in, but that's a very expensive luxury these days. In a worst-case scenario, the student may ultimately realize that she would like to study something not even offered at the school she is attending! She'll have to transfer to a different college, and probably lose credits in the process, which compounds the already exorbitant cost of college attendance.

══COLLEGE BY THE NUMBERS══

According to the U.S. Department of Education's National Center for Education Statistics, students who attended one college took an average of fifty-one months to graduate, while students who attended two schools took an extra eight months to reach that milestone. Students who attended three or more colleges took an average of sixty-seven months to reach graduation, which is a huge hit in the pocketbook for both family and student. Those extra months add up to a lot of extra money, while increasing the likelihood that a student may become discouraged and never attain a degree at all.

─────────── $ ───────────

One way of reducing college costs is for everyone concerned—you, the student, and you, the parents—to make the career choice very carefully. Solid career choices lead to smart college choices, thus speeding up time to graduation. This is a big money saver for everyone!

Focus on the Meaningful Things

Many prospective college students focus on superficial concerns when making a college selection. Where is the school located? Where are my friends going? Do I like the campus? What is the social life like? Often, you put off career concerns until *after* you enroll. It is almost as though students and their families believe that career plans will somehow miraculously unfold during college.

Perhaps they will, but they may not. It is true that some students will find their career passions in college. I emphasize, however, this is only *some*. A few students will also make helpful connections in college that will lead to jobs afterward, although paradoxically, the networking value of college appears to be declining somewhat as the number of students increases. (This may also have to do with the growth of social media, which offers a valuable alternate network.) Many students unfortunately graduate with little understanding of the working world and their place in it. In some cases, college can actually serve to insulate them from basic economic realities. For instance, college often shields students from the true costs of their education, since parents assume financial responsibilities and payments are delayed on student loans.

There are no easy shortcuts when it comes to career planning. Coming to a career decision requires a great deal of exploration and reflection. Part-time jobs have an important role to play in discovering your interests and abilities, which is another reason you should look carefully for employment opportunities while you're in school.

THE THIEL FELLOWSHIP

Peter Thiel, the founder of PayPal, has come forward and famously offered substantial grants, called Thiel Fellowships, to a few promising students to work on entrepreneurial ventures. However, a condition of receiving the grant is that the student must leave college. Thiel's view is that "education has become a way to avoid thinking about your future. Instead of thinking about your future, you go to school and defer thinking about your life."

Whether or not you agree with Thiel's program, you can see that the mindset he's talking about is precisely one that students must *not* adopt. College can be a means of getting where you want to go, but in order for it to work effectively, you have to have some idea of where you are heading.

HOW SHOULD YOU PLAN YOUR CAREER?

All too often, a teenager's interests are all over the map. Many of their ideas have not begun to merge by high school graduation. More than a few teens will need a helpful nudge from well-meaning adults to begin to narrow down suitable and realistic career options. It is important to assess shifts in the labor force, as you weigh your alternatives.

High schools tend to promote college as the next step for the overwhelming majority of their students, thereby kicking the problem further along the path. It's almost as if they see going to college as a career choice for these students. Your family may well be struggling with career planning, as well. After all, as parents you are normally only familiar with a few jobs, yourselves. You may want to leave this exploration process to the academic professionals and be hands off. This can be a big mistake; students with unclear occupational plans when they enter college have a way of returning home later as unemployed college graduates, towing hefty educational bills behind them.

HELP YOUR TEEN MAKE INFORMED CAREER CHOICES

You may not want to interfere with your children's decision-making process and force career choices on them. While this is noble, it can turn out to be expensive, and the results are mixed.

It is worth pointing out that not all cultures are as reticent as ours about pointing a child toward certain careers. For example,

Asian and Indian parents are often rather prescriptive in determining a child's career path, and their children tend to enjoy relatively high levels of occupational and economic success.

How can you, as parents, help students to career success without squashing individuality and self-determination? And how can you, as students, make the best career choice possible?

The answer is to follow your student's natural interests and abilities, to research related career opportunities, and to inject strong doses of reality, as required, as the student's interests develop. Parents shouldn't be afraid to offer some direction and constructive feedback along the way; most children truly need and appreciate this. And, students, if you think your parents are way off base, speak up. You'll open the door to an important discussion.

Learn about Yourself

Fundamentally, all career development involves first learning about yourself and then learning about the working world. Personal traits, interests, and aptitudes tend to be fairly fixed, whereas the working world is always evolving. In recent years, it has been undergoing such major shifts that even many adults have been blindsided by the enormous changes.

Many teens do not know themselves well, yet, and they know even less about the labor market. For students who lack strong interests and self-awareness, the career exploration process is especially crucial. This is one reason why it can make good sense to delay college matriculation when a student is completely undecided about career direction. Colleges are generally quite willing to grant requests for "gap years" for admitted students, and most students who take a break before college benefit greatly from the experience. It can save you a lot of money, in the long run, if a student develops career focus before enrolling as a freshman.

It is beneficial for all students to understand employment trends during periods of high unemployment. In a recession, it's especially important that you closely evaluate the employment market, because there's a limited supply of jobs. Where do experts predict that jobs will be plentiful in the future? This is a great place to begin a career search if you're unclear about your career aspirations or concerned about employment. For information on employment trends, go to the Bureau of Labor Statistics (*www.bls.gov*).

Be Realistic

We all need to be realistic in our employment expectations right now, given the current job statistics. The working world is changing dramatically, and it is becoming harder and harder for adults to find and maintain middle-class jobs. That's doubly true for new entrants to the workforce. Parents and counselors are not doing students any favors by allowing them to harbor unrealistic career fantasies in severe economic conditions.

To find factual and reliable career information to help guide the decision-making process, I recommend visiting the government's own websites featuring information gathered by the U.S. Department of Labor. This is some of the most recent and comprehensive information you will find. At *www.careeronestop* *.org* and *www.onetonline.org* you can:

- **Access vast resources on careers**

- **Conduct searches of different career options using various parameters**

- Find documentation on virtually every job under the sun, including descriptions of what each occupation entails, the daily tasks required, and the education necessary to enter the field

- Find helpful information on salaries and benefits (essential for reality testing) along with projections on the numbers of openings to expect in the future

The only way to find better career information is to speak directly to individuals working in fields of interest. They have access to the very latest, insider knowledge.

Predicting the future is always difficult; the best we have to go on are concrete historical statistics coupled with wisdom and common sense. There are some larger patterns in the economy, mainly driven by demographics, that we can foresee and that are more reliable than shorter-term economic trends. For example, the aging baby boomer generation will be retiring soon, creating a huge, inevitable demand for certain services, such as health care. Likewise, public school and college faculties are rapidly aging, and a large wave of retirements is expected. These are the sorts of labor trends to notice.

Most high school graduates focus primarily on deciding which institution to attend after high school. Because they have a short-range perspective, they tend to focus only on the *next* decision that faces them: college. Their thoughts about career become secondary. In fact, you'll spend only a few years in college but the rest of your life in your career, so the career choice obviously deserves priority.

Do a Reality Check

Parents need to talk to their college-bound students about careers. It is a mistake to assume that guidance counselors or college advisers will do this for you. You should also reality test your child. Point out certain occupations and ask how much he thinks they pay. Ask how much he thinks *you* earn. Many of you will be astounded by how much your high school student's ideas of salary vary from reality. You need to correct these mistaken assumptions before students make major educational decisions, such as selecting a college program.

All college students should also regularly reality check and update their own career assumptions. Visit *www.careeronestop .org* or *www.salary.com* to learn what high school teachers actually earn compared to lawyers or nurses and what the projected job outlook is for each of these careers. Even when you are set on a certain career path, it helps tremendously to know if opportunities in your chosen field are currently limited or expanding and the level of salary to expect; this information empowers you to tailor your job search and financial strategies accordingly.

Parents, you should also explain how much it costs, month by month, to support the entire family. The student's (and family's) future economic survival is at stake; don't be afraid to force the issue of career planning before signing up to foot the bill for four or more years of college tuition based on nothing more than high hopes, a few glossy marketing brochures, and a pleasant campus tour.

REALITY RULE #3

OLD RULE:	NEW RULE:
Focus on your GPA in college to ensure you get hired.	*Focus on the job market to ensure you get hired.*

Ironically, being an excellent student can sometimes hurt your chances of finding career success. This is because when you focus excessively on grades and schoolwork you can lose sight of the real world, a world that will enable you to recognize, prepare for, and take advantage of emerging opportunities.

I recently had lunch with a friend of mine, who went back to graduate school after a divorce. She had just completed her degree and was not having any luck getting employers to respond to her job applications. She lamented the fact that she had spent the past few years with her head in a book and, as she put it, "lost touch with the outside world." She had earned excellent grades, but they weren't helping her to land a job. During her academic program, she failed to stay in contact with her personal and professional network, and now she was struggling to rebuild those connections and get noticed by those with the power to hire her.

You're rewarded, from a very early age, for doing good work in school. The problem is that at some point school ends and real life begins. When you get to that stage, you need to be able to move from studying about the world to working in it. Educators are often of limited assistance in offering advice on how to make this transition, as they stay immersed in the world of academia, while you must leave.

CAREER PREPARATION 101

It's odd that "C" students sometimes seem to understand career planning better than the "A" students. Perhaps, because the average students don't love doing schoolwork as much as the top scholars, they spend more time "peeking out the window" and planning for their post-college lives. Top students are so accustomed to being recognized for their superior academic performance that they think the more they study, the more they will be rewarded in life. Many of these strong students are in for a very bumpy transition to the workforce. This is not how the real world works. The real world rewards those who can recognize economic opportunities and take action.

The *Harvard Crimson* used to devote its last page to what it called "The Real World." The rest of the student newspaper focused on the goings-on around campus—presumably the "unreal world." But the last page briefly summarized snippets of the major news stories of the day that the rest of the world was following. This is probably the way a lot of students look at the "real world." As I hope I've made clear, I think this is a mistake. This awareness needs to be present throughout the student's college years and come into sharp focus as she or he nears graduation. The closer you get to that important day, the more you must focus on broader issues and economic concerns.

Therefore, as a college student, part of your employment strategy is developing familiarity with existing career opportunities and how to access them when college is finished. You need to pay attention to your own marketability: How do you provide something valuable that other people will want to buy? This means participating in the real economy by having paying jobs and learning firsthand what rates employers are willing to offer for certain types of services and talents. This is precisely the sort of information you will *not* be gaining if you focus most of your out-of-class energy on unpaid community service events or volunteer activities, because these activities do not involve economic transactions.

The Importance of High School Jobs

Career preparation also means building a professional image—represented on a growing resume—to increase the chances of being hired. I believe that every high school senior should create a resume in preparation for college admissions. This is a great exercise in developing personal and career awareness. This goes hand in hand with my belief that high school students should get jobs while they're in school. (Because so few high school students work these days, admissions committees now view jobs held in high school very favorably. This is great news for those of you who have to work for your own spending money.)

Producing a resume can also provide a much-needed wakeup call to a young adult who may suddenly realize that he has nothing concrete to list in terms of employment. This student then sees the need to use the opportunities during college to accumulate experiences and references to flesh out his professional presentation.

Furthermore, getting a job in high school is good practice for getting into college and for getting a job afterward. In many ways, the hiring process mirrors the college admissions process. You must present yourself to an organization, made up of individuals, in such a way as to make them want to make you an offer to join them.

Colleges look for students who stand out. Some ways to get noticed include:

- **Having a special talent no one else has**
- **Being from an underrepresented group or location**
- **Having achieved distinction in a favorite area of interest**

All of these factors can help with college admissions, and are sometimes referred to as "hooks" because they can help you reel in the admissions offer. Throughout the entire admissions process, it is extremely important to focus on the desires of the audience, in this case the admissions committee, in order to position yourself optimally and improve your chances.

Employers, whether you're in high school or after you've graduated college, are also looking for applicants who stand out, but they consider different factors. Again, it is crucial to focus on the needs and desires of the intended audience when presenting yourself for consideration. Yes, they want to see that you completed college with a respectable academic record, but most employers don't require straight "A" students. Instead, they look for relevant work experience and enthusiastic letters of recommendation from respected individuals. Letters of recommendation from professors are good, but references from former employers are even better—particularly if the people doing the hiring know the references personally. Best of all are professional contacts within the targeted firm who can offer a personal endorsement. This is why networking is so important, throughout college and beyond.

DEVELOPING A PERSONAL BRAND

Both in applying to college and searching for a job, you can benefit from what has been termed personal *branding* or *positioning*. The term *branding* refers to the way that we learn to recognize and pick one particular brand item off the store shelf rather than another. We do this because the product we prefer communicates to us that it is going to meet our needs better than any other competing option.

Positioning yourself for college admissions can provide great preparation for branding yourself for employment, although the specific message must shift according to your audience. The same strategies that can help you get into a good college can be adapted to help you find a great job afterward.

Brands for high school-aged college applicants are different from brands you'll develop when you're looking for a job after graduation, but with both you must primarily consider the view of the audience. Through high school, you developed a track record of success that will hopefully make colleges want to accept you. This consists mainly of your grades and teacher recommendations, which are what colleges require.

This is the beginning of a brand, but throughout college you'll refine it in ways that will eventually appeal to desirable employers. Job-seeking brands need to be more professional and more closely aligned with the workforce than with school. This is where many college students miss the boat. They are still immersed in the educational world and think that they will be hired based on their grades and extracurricular activities, since that is what helped them to gain admission to college.

When you apply to college or for a job, *you* are the product that you must convince other people to select. To succeed, you must demonstrate that you have something compelling to offer that the other options do not. There are many brands of soap on the shelf to buy, and there are many college and job applicants from which admissions officers and employers can select. How are you going to get them to notice you?

Grab their attention by showing them that you already know what they want and that you have what they are looking for. This requires understanding the audience—in this case, potential employers—well and demonstrating that you possess the capabilities to meet their needs through your resume and other branding materials you create and supply. When they scan the pile of applicants, they can see immediately that you are the right choice to select.

Applying Online

Increasingly, job applications are moving beyond the traditional resume to include online components. For instance, you can expect potential employers to conduct a Google search of the applicants they are considering for a position. One way to eliminate yourself from contention is to have a negative online presence, such as unflattering public Facebook posts. But don't go to the extreme of not having any online presence at all. Today, many employers look for employees with positive online visibility, through websites, blogs, and social media. They like applicants with large established networks or followings. Personal branding expert Dan Schawbel believes that every jobseeker needs to create a consistent and appealing social media presence using online tools such as Facebook, LinkedIn, Twitter, and a blog to advertise his capabilities and differentiate him from competitors. This presence must be a coherent part of the personal brand you are developing. Ideally, it will include demonstrations of your abilities, a track record of success, and key endorsements from respected individuals.

Schawbel also advises college students to build a strong network *before* you need it, rather than waiting until senior year— or worse, after graduation—to begin. My point is that all of this hard work takes place outside of the college classroom . . . and it can really pay off.

Unless you are applying to graduate school, grades are unlikely to be a major factor in your hiring, and extracurricular activities will probably only help if they're related to the job you are seeking. Employers are looking for employees with useful skills, demonstrated capabilities, a visible track record of success, and impressive endorsements. Developing all of these attributes is as important, if not more important, than maximizing your grade-point average. The reality is that college GPAs do not matter as much when seeking an entry-level job as high school GPAs matter for college admission.

Don't focus so much on classes and grades that you fail to prepare adequately for post-college employment. Getting a job is the real final exam! Students need to step outside the Ivory Tower regularly to ensure that they familiarize themselves with the expectations of real world employers and the functioning economy.

Especially during economic recessions, you must pay close attention to the changing job market to ensure you are positioning yourself to be employed quickly after graduation. Don't let being a good student today stand in the way of the future. Focusing on grades is a short-term concern that can cause some diligent students to lose focus on the real prize—the long-term goal of finding a great job that pays well.

CHAPTER 3

VISITING CAMPUSES AND EVALUATING YOUR COLLEGE CHOICES

REALITY RULE # 4

OLD RULE:	NEW RULE:
Begin college visits in the Admissions Office.	*Begin college visits in the Career Center.*

I f you've read Stephen Covey's bestselling book *Seven Habits of Highly Effective People*, you may remember that he advises you to begin with the end in mind. This sage piece of advice is particularly apt when you're engaged in the college selection process. Without a doubt, the most cost-effective means of selecting the right college, which serves a student's intended purposes, is to have a clear exit strategy before entering. If you're concerned with employment—and you should be, whether you're the student or the parent—this means having career goals in mind.

The more focused a student is about her career objectives upon starting college, the more likely she will be to extract the maximum value from the experience and to achieve her goals upon commencement. Too often, students avoid career planning as more immediate and enjoyable distractions take precedence: Viewbooks! Campus visits! Dorm tours! Overnight stays! Students tend to postpone career plans until some distant future time when those concerns suddenly must move center stage. At that point, a college upperclassman may suddenly realize that she is on the wrong track altogether.

Your college planning process will be different. Yes, you are going to take the college tour, register in the admissions office, and participate in question-answer sessions. But you are going to make one important stop that 99.5 percent of other prospective students and families will never think to make: *you are also going to visit the career center.*

WELCOME TO THE CAREER CENTER!

The typical college student won't visit the college's career center until senior year. Of course, the typical college student also begins working on a term paper the night before it's due. Obviously, if you want the results to be good, this is far too late to begin. To get the edge on the competition, you need to begin sooner (both visiting the career center *and* writing your term papers).

The career center is the place to begin—not end—a college career. This visit and discussion will make a huge impression on high school seniors. Students need to understand that the career center is for all four years of college, not just the last few months. During your initial visit, inquire about the employment rates of graduates and learn what job-search assistance will be available for senior year and summer breaks.

You probably won't have any trouble getting attention as a visitor in the career center, unless you are visiting during spring recruiting season when the current crop of graduating seniors is panicking. It is typically one of the most underused services on campus. If it is busy when you are there, that's a good sign. It means students on this campus take their job prospects seriously. On the other hand, a quiet career center can mean you'll receive lots of personalized attention, particularly during the fall or winter, or even over the summer.

BETTER LATE THAN NEVER!

Oddly enough, alumni are one of the growing populations using college career services. Talk about procrastination! This trend is so strong that some colleges are even adding alumni wings to their career centers. While it is admirable that colleges are taking responsibility for assisting their graduates in finding or switching careers years later, it is also a bit disconcerting that they need to do so.

Career planning in collaboration with the career center is one of the very best ways to save money on college. If you've got a strong career plan, you're unlikely to make the very costly decision to switch majors three or four times. You're more likely to make good course selections and to see a guiding purpose behind all your academic and extracurricular endeavors. This will contribute to making the entire college experience more meaningful. That end goal—a career aspiration—is what provides much of the motivation to carry out the hard work of college.

By all means visit the admissions office. Admissions representatives are great people who will be more than happy to see you. They will answer your questions honestly and be helpful and welcoming. It's just that everything is always rosy in the admissions office, and there is only so much information you can find there. This is the front entrance to a college. You want to see what's going on closer to the exit—"backstage," as it were.

Stop in the career center and look around. Inquire about how many career counselors they have and find out something about their backgrounds. Ask about the placement rates of graduates in the majors you are considering and listen to their answers. I would be saddened, but not surprised, if many colleges cannot tell you about the placement rates of their graduates. Few collect this sort of information, despite growing calls for colleges to document their outcomes so that consumers can make more-informed decisions.

As you visit more college career offices, you will begin to notice considerable differences in the levels of activity and the resources available. Some colleges and even universities only have a single career counselor for the entire student body! Others rely on students to conduct most of what passes for career counseling. The variation in resources should be an important consideration in your college selection process.

CHAPTER 4

TAKING RESPONSIBILITY FOR YOUR EDUCATION

REALITY RULE #5

OLD RULE:	NEW RULE:
You will "feel" which college is right when you visit.	*Choose a college with your head, not your heart.*

A dolescents tend to "think" and "reason" emotionally. The intuitive side of the typical teenage brain leads the way, and the rational intellectual processes go along for the ride. Yet, in many cases, it is these same young people who are making most of the college decisions in this country—decisions regarding hundreds of thousands of dollars, in many cases.

Imagine you're standing side by side with your daughter. In front of you is a new car lot; next to it is a high-end jewelry store. You hand her your credit card and say, "Pick out absolutely anything you want. Don't even look at the cost! There's no limit, and I'll pick up the bill."

No right-thinking parent would do this, yet every day parents take their kids on college tours with the implication that "money is no object" and "the sky is the limit." If money really isn't a problem for you, congratulations! Be my guest and purchase all the college you can afford. The rest of us, however, need to watch our wallets and consider our education choices more carefully.

This essentially irrational process is helped along by the conventional wisdom that advises teens to visit colleges until they find the one that "feels" right. The student presumably knows, when he or she walks on campus, that this is the "right" school for him or her. It could be the way the trees wave in the breeze, the handsome guys or cute girls who pass by, or even just the way the tour guide looks or speaks. It could just be the weather on the particular day you visit or the selections in the dining hall that afternoon. But . . . whatever it is, the emotional decision is made, their hearts are set, and all that is left is for the parents to find a way to make the financing happen.

Colleges understand that emotions play a large part in the college selection process, and they take advantage of this at every turn. From football teams to fight songs and from mascots to picturesque campuses, colleges are expert at stirring young (and old) emotions. Today, they even begin building brand loyalty at birth, with cute onesies, bibs, and sippy cups emblazoned with school logos and "Future Member of the Class of 20__." After a childhood adorned in such spiritwear, how could any heartless parent deprive a child of the lifelong dream school? It's unthinkable! Price becomes no object.

To be very clear here: I am *not* suggesting to parents that you make all the college decisions for your child. That would be counterproductive and would lead to a lot more trouble than it would prevent. What I am suggesting is that making a decision about the college-bound aspirations of a student should be a *mutual* decision arrived at between parent and future student. Make the decision together, based on a rational evaluation of family finances and the student's career aspirations, and you'll avoid plenty of heartache and wallet-ache along the way.

SPUR OF THE MOMENT DECISIONS

College, believe it or not, can even be an impulse purchase, as first-generation college student Kelli Space, who now owes $200,000 in loans on her bachelor's degree in sociology from Northeastern, learned the hard way. Space, who has been open about sharing her college debt story in the media, now acknowledges that she made a poor financial decision in selecting her college; she simply bought the wishful hype that money shouldn't keep her from going to the school of her dreams. Now, she is facing a financial nightmare, likely to last decades and to limit her life options in early adulthood. (More about her situation later.)

Colleges take advantage of the inexperience of youth as well as the selflessness of parents, who are frequently unwilling to deny their children the very best—even when they have no idea how they will possibly pay for it all. To parents feeling this pressure, I encourage you to picture your college student coming back to you after graduation, waving unaffordable loan statements and asking, "Why did you let me do this?" If you're willing to assume the college debt for your children, try picturing them asking instead, "How am I supposed to pay for your retirement?"

Emotion

There are many reasons why some students and families make ill-advised economic decisions regarding college, but emotions are certainly one of the biggest. Families want to give their children the best possible start in life, and traditionally this has meant going to college. Another reason is because the costs are now so staggering that they are difficult to comprehend. Many families simply go into shutdown mode and enter pure denial when it is time to discuss the real costs involved.

Social Class

Social class is also a big consideration in the college decision. The undisputed value of attending college, and even going into debt to do so, has long been a central part of the middle-class belief system. Questioning it can unleash a great deal of anxiety and even anger. Parents fear that their children may lose perceived social standing unless they attend college—no matter the cost. The middle classes generally sense that they are losing their precarious foothold in the economy and continue to believe that having children who are college graduates is a sign of prosperity, even when it may now, in fact, be a sign of the exact opposite: penury.

There is almost nothing families will not sacrifice to attain the college dream. Therefore, emotions tend to override rational thinking, even for parents, when college and children are involved.

Colleges count on this devotion and generally rely on emotional appeals to market their programs, rather than economic ones. Also, as increasing numbers of parents are themselves college graduates, it becomes harder to question making this same investment on behalf of the next generation—even when there is considerable evidence indicating that the payoff from a college degree has declined significantly. As a college planner, I frequently notice how enthused parents become when I speak publicly on the topic of gaining admission to college . . . and how quickly their eyes glaze over at any mention of economic or workforce realities. Most would prefer not to consider those issues.

In Florida, recently, I spotted an alarming TV commercial selling the college dream to first-generation Hispanic students. Against a picture of a modest one-story home with a pickup truck in the driveway, a young man's voice announces to his mother that he has received a job offer and wants to take it. The mother replies, "No, you're going to college." "It's a good job," the young man counters. "Anyway, it's my decision." "Yes," the mother replies, "it's your decision. You get to decide what you're going to major in, because you're going to college."

A voiceover announcer then counsels that it is the duty of Hispanic parents to tell their children to go to college, despite their protests. Meanwhile, as the announcer speaks, the video of the one-story home magically transforms itself into an upscale colonial while the pickup truck changes into a luxury sedan. The message is simple and clear: Go to college like your mother says and all your materialistic dreams will somehow miraculously come true.

When I saw this commercial, I wondered: What are the odds this fictional student will find himself back in his parents' one-story ranch home in four or five years without a job but instead with a $600-per-month student loan payment he cannot make?

With media messages like these, it's no wonder that young, impressionable eighteen-year-olds buy wholeheartedly into the college dream without question or thought.

KEEP YOUR FEET ON THE GROUND

Now that college costs are so high, college cannot be handled solely as an emotional decision; it must also be a prudent, rational one. I hope that the parents reading this book enjoy your college visits with your child, but I advise you to keep your emotions in check and hold tightly on to your checkbook. Remember that there is no single college option that will make or break her future. My grandfather used to remind me that, "knowledge has no address." A hard-working, motivated student will be able to grow intellectually and find success wherever she goes to college. At one time, it really did matter if students attended college in a certain location where the esteemed library held rare and hard-to-access volumes of necessary information. This is no longer true; the Internet now makes it easy to retrieve information from anywhere in the world.

It's possible if the student needs access to highly specialized resources and personal contacts in narrow fields of expertise, she might consider attending a particular school that provides these resources. But at the undergraduate level, each state has a variety of satisfactory options for students of all ability levels.

SATISFICING OUR NEEDS

Another principle to keep in mind when choosing a college comes to us from the economist Herbert Simon, who proposed the principle of *satisficing*. A blend of "satisfy" and "suffice," the term means that there are many acceptable solutions to a problem, and that sometimes the "optimum" choice will prove no more satisfactory than an adequate one. College, like a vehicle, is merely a means of getting where you want to go. In ordinary circumstances, a person can generally travel just as quickly and just as far in a Ford as in a Lamborghini, but at considerably less cost. Remind yourself that financial security is the greatest luxury item of all and don't be persuaded to buy more college than you need or can comfortably afford.

REALITY RULE #6

OLD RULE:	NEW RULE:
Count on your adviser to map out a course schedule and plan of study.	*Double-check everything a college adviser tells you.*

One of the key strategies for reducing college costs is to move through college quickly. Though this is a preferred course of action, the horrifying fact is that, as costs rise, American college students are taking even longer to graduate than ever before. This is unacceptable and unaffordable.

This generation of college students seems to have grown comfortable with the notion that college should take longer than four years to complete. The majority of students, these days, seem to be on the five-year plan. In reality, the idea of the four-year baccalaureate program has always been arbitrary, and it is not fixed in stone. It is quite possible to graduate from college in a shorter timeframe by accelerating an academic program.

Parents, don't let your child join the majority of students who fail to graduate on time. Students, don't add to your college costs by taking more time than is necessary to complete your course of study. The average family simply cannot afford this. With tuition costs as high as they are, college students need to focus on graduating more quickly, not more slowly. They need to get in, earn their credits, and get out as fast as possible, so that their debts are reduced and their parents can continue saving for a secure retirement. To make this happen, students must be efficient in course selection and completion.

COLLEGE BY THE NUMBERS

Here is a shocking statistic: A recent report by the Education Trust found that only 37 percent of first-year freshmen entering four-year baccalaureate programs completed their degrees within the standard four years. Of course, added time means additional costs. For each additional year, students are heaping 25 percent or more to their already staggering college costs by failing to accumulate the necessary credits to receive their diplomas in a timely fashion.

$

As well, consider the opportunity cost of spending extra time in college. Those extra semesters don't just mean more tuition money; they also delay your entry into the workforce. Think about that. Every week you're in college is one week you could be at work, drawing a paycheck.

TAKE RESPONSIBILITY

The quickest way through college is to take full responsibility for planning your own course schedule. Most students embarking on a college degree have been trained in passivity by thirteen years of elementary and high school behavior modification. In fact, you may have been punished for showing too much initiative and questioning safe assumptions. You are accustomed to letting adults tell you what to do regarding your schooling, so you typically wait to receive their instructions.

If this sounds like you, you're probably following the same path of least resistance when planning your college programs. Most college students count on their academic advisers to map out their course schedules. This is pretty much how high school works, where guidance counselors assume most of the responsibility for ensuring that students graduate on time.

Well, guess what? Your college academic adviser doesn't care how quickly you graduate. Your earlier education was free (if you attended public school) but college costs a fortune. Once the bills shift to you, so must the initiative.

You're Responsible Now!

This is ultimately a lesson about assuming personal responsibility. Students and parents who master the course registration process can use a variety of strategies to cut semesters or even years off of the time it takes to graduate from college, which can ultimately slash tens of thousands of dollars off the final tuition bill. It's obviously well worth the investment of time and effort to make the best possible selections. It could wind up saving you big time.

Be alert, read the fine print, and take charge of planning a streamlined college course of study. As we shall see, students and their parents should really begin this process in high school to maximize potential savings, because today there are many opportunities to begin racking up valuable college credits before high school graduation. The earlier you start, and the more thoroughly you understand the requirements, the more quickly you can be receiving that college diploma.

PLANNING A COURSE OF STUDY

Strategic course planning is essential to gaining control of exorbitant college costs. Here is how it works: When you start college, you're assigned to an adviser. If you know what you plan to major in, you will probably be supplied with an adviser in the area of interest, but undecided students might receive a temporary adviser from any field.

The quality of these advisers varies tremendously. Some are seasoned professors with years of experience. They are adept in guiding young people to the best courses that meet important requirements so that they can graduate in the expected period of time. They are cost-sensitive and realize that, when it comes to college, time is money. They remind students of important enrollment deadlines to ensure that they are able to find seats in the classes they need to progress steadily. They follow up with students regularly and wouldn't dream of steering students to courses that do not fulfill mandatory steps to graduation.

Other advisers are not as good. They may be young and inexperienced. They may be new to the institution and unfamiliar with its rules, regulations, and programs of study. They may be adept in their area of academic specialty, but terrible at advising. Most college professors, it should be noted, are not relieved of other duties in order to devote themselves to advising. In fact, advising duties tend to be despised by many faculty members. It is quite common for senior faculty members to dump these responsibilities on overburdened junior faculty members at many universities. These swamped advisers may inadvertently —or sometimes deliberately—advise students to sign up for courses that will not count toward graduation or degree completion. Whether it is through ignorance or not, these advisers, despite their name, may not offer the best advice.

Occasionally, advisers will steer students toward courses taught by themselves or preferred colleagues, to ensure that the numbers in these courses stay up, thus providing themselves with greater job security. They may encourage students to take courses that the advisers believe the students should take, regardless of the effect on time to graduation or the students' economic status. Sometimes, they may be insensitive to students' financial constraints and forget that some students cannot afford any scheduling errors. Poor advisers may also fail to follow up with students, allowing them to miss important deadlines, lose seats in necessary courses, and throw an entire plan of study off schedule. These sorts of mistakes happen all the time.

Don't Take It for Granted

The adage that applies here is, "Trust, but verify." Listen to what the adviser says, but double-check and confirm every detail, independently. Graduation requirements change all the time and advisers are busy people. They may overlook details or miss potential shortcuts. Remember this: A college plan of study is like a contract. This contract states in writing that if you fulfill the terms, the school must award you a degree. The terms state exactly what you must do in order to receive the coveted diploma. A plan of study contract should be approached with the seriousness of any other legal document binding you to pay large amounts of money. Study it thoroughly and read the fine print.

This past month, I experienced the importance of this rule firsthand as my own college-bound daughter attended orientation and attempted to negotiate her first semester schedule with her assigned adviser. Repeatedly, this adviser signed her up for courses for which she had already received AP credits and enrolled her in the wrong levels of courses. If we had not caught her mistakes, these courses would have been complete wastes of time. It took no less than seven rounds of scheduling, via e-mail over the summer, before we were finally able to ensure that there were no unnecessary courses on my daughter's schedule.

My daughter was understandably bewildered and exasperated by the experience, and exclaimed more than once, "How am I supposed to know how this works? Isn't she supposed to figure this out for me?" You would think so, but don't count on it.

I'm not trying to make a villain out of this particular adviser. Now that I think about it, I realize that she is responsible for advising all the new students in the honors college at this state university. That is over 100 incoming students. There simply is no way she can maximize the opportunities for every single one.

The lesson here is that no one will ever care about the schedule as much as the individual student. So, it is up to you to read the rules and ask the right questions. Students and families who fail to read the plan of study and graduation requirements are similar to people who sign a mortgage agreeing to pay hundreds of thousands of dollars, with interest, without reviewing or understanding the terms. Don't do it!

BE PREPARED

By studying the requirements for graduation as outlined in course catalogs and other official university documents, you can learn how to get from Point A (enrollment) to Point B (graduation) in the shortest time possible. This is a crucial life lesson that will serve you well in other arenas. Unfortunately, many—probably most—students fail to do this. They count on their adviser to steer them in the right direction.

First-generation college students are probably most susceptible to this mistake, as they do not have parents experienced in the college process to offer practical guidance and helpful insights. Instead, when these unprepared students show up to meet with their advisers, they often arrive as blank slates, with equally blank registration cards.

Anyone listening might witness the following exchange:

"What courses are you looking to take this semester?"

The student shrugs, and looks at the adviser expectantly.

"I dunno. What do you suggest?"

This is like walking into a car salesman's office and telling him you need a new car but don't know what kind you want. Before you know it, you are loaded up on the latest model with all the coolest accessories and with an overloaded price to match.

There is a disclaimer buried in most college course catalogs absolving the institution and adviser of responsibility if the program of study fails to help a student to progress toward graduation. Here's one example of this wording: "Final responsibility for each student's program of study rests with the student. The role of the adviser is just that—to advise. Students are expected to familiarize themselves thoroughly with program requirements for their major."

The college is protecting itself for good reason. College students and advisers make huge, costly mistakes in planning courses all the time.

The smartest families will sit down with their student, the course catalogs, and the list of degree requirements and plan out an entire year's worth of courses *before* the student goes to the adviser. Better yet, plan out all four years of college—the entire program of study! Be ruthless about it. This is a student's life energy and your collective financial future at stake. The college is certainly going to be willing to let a student take extra, unnecessary courses along the way because they make more money that way. It is up to you to cut out anything that is nonessential to reduce your costs.

Bear in mind that students can also request to change their advisers and should certainly do so if they find that their adviser is unhelpful, slow to respond to questions, or generally ill-informed. It pays to ask other students for their recommendations on which advisers are best.

Long-Term Planning Is Best

Long-term course planning is increasingly essential, as state budget cuts and increased enrollments are making it harder for students at many public institutions to find spaces in classes. Course availability tends to be one area where private colleges can offer an advantage over public ones. Many private colleges will advertise that although their cost of attendance is considerably higher, they guarantee their students will be able to enroll in all the courses necessary to graduate within the expected four-year timeframe.

It is true that students at public colleges often face greater difficulty in getting into courses. However, it is still possible to graduate in four years from a public college, though it may require careful planning on your part. Keep in mind, though, that a less expensive school is no bargain if it takes much longer to get through. Those additional semesters will quickly consume your cost savings.

Many college students do not realize that they need to take such a high level of initiative with their course planning. They sit politely and passively and wait for their adviser or another adult to tell them what to do. They change their majors without considering the economic implications of that choice. Many of these students will not realize their mistake until sophomore or even junior year, when they discover that they have been taking many courses but are still miles away from earning a degree. At this point they may become discouraged, give up, and drop out. Proactive planning can prevent this outcome. Steady progress toward a degree is essential for maintaining academic motivation.

Give Your Student the Help She Needs

Parents, you may need to take the lead in explaining to a new freshman how to read a course catalog and plan a course of study. Of course, this is easier if you've had some college experience of your own, but anyone with determination can do it. The prospect of paying the cost for a fifth year of tuition, which a majority of students and parents now do, ought to be all the motivation you need to tackle this crucial task.

HIGH SCHOOL SENIORS ARE THE NEW COLLEGE FRESHMEN

Today, it's possible for motivated students to start accumulating college credits before they even receive their high school diplomas. Advanced Placement tests and International Baccalaureate programs are two of the best ways to reduce the cost of college. In some cases, bright students can knock tens of thousands of dollars off their college bills before setting foot on campus!

AP and IB

Advanced Placement (AP) and International Baccalaureate (IB) courses are college-level courses that are taught in high schools. AP courses are more familiar in the United States. These courses used to be reserved for high school seniors, but juniors and even some sophomores now take them. They are among the best college bargains you'll ever find.

Using college-level textbooks, students in an AP course will complete the equivalent of a college course curriculum in high school. At the end of the year, students take an AP test to determine if they have attained a level of knowledge equivalent to what would be expected in a college course. The test scores range from 1 to 5; students who receive scores between 3 and 5 typically receive at least three college credits for their efforts. Some AP courses carry as many as eight college credits for a high score!

The cost to earn three college credits can range anywhere from a few hundred dollars at a community college to several thousand at an elite school. Students who begin accumulating AP credits in high school can sock away a year's worth of courses—or more—before beginning college. At a high-priced private school, that is worth a cool $50,000. Is there any doubt that your student had better crack open those AP study guides? You can pick them up at most bookstores for around $20.

Even better, students can actually take AP tests without even taking the related AP course! The Educational Testing Service doesn't generally advertise this fact, but home-schooled students do it all the time. My own daughter did this her junior year, and scored a 5 on an AP test with a few hours of self-study. For her effort, she will receive six credits at her number-one college choice and can now skip two basic introductory courses. If you have a bright student who tests well, some self-study with an AP prep guide might result in a passing score. The only cost of taking the test is a modest registration fee of about $80.

You should review your intended college's policy on accepting AP credits as you sign up for these courses and tests. For example, one high school junior received a score of 5 on the English Language & Composition AP Test. He then checked with his chosen college and discovered that this counted for the maximum number of English AP credits available. He then realized that it made no sense to take the senior class in AP Literature, as he was planning to do, and he signed up for AP History, instead.

Some AP courses carry far more credits than others at particular colleges. So, do your homework early on to make the best decisions. Most college websites post official policies on accepting AP credits. You should use this information to guide high school course selection. Every family that is serious about sending a child to college and saving money should take full advantage of the AP and IB opportunities available in secondary school.

CLEP Tests

An even better-kept secret on the college level is the CLEP test, which stands for College Level Examination Program. Colleges generally do not broadcast the availability of this testing option, and for good reason. For just $77, a college student can take a test to demonstrate competency in a subject area. If he passes the test, he can earn from three to twelve college credits, saving himself thousands in tuition while shaving time off his degree program. Every college student in America should be looking into this! This is a great opportunity for adult students with years of accumulated knowledge and experience. You can find comprehensive testing guides to help you prepare for these examinations. Check your college's website and course catalog to determine their policy on awarding CLEP credits. You can also find out more about the CLEP test at *www.collegeboard.com.*

Dual Enrollment

Dual enrollment classes provide another great opportunity to save on college. A dual enrollment class allows a student to take a course at a nearby college (or community college) and receive both high school and college credit for it. Often, these courses are offered at no cost to the student. Even the price of the textbook may be covered! Dual enrollment classes can dramatically reduce the time to obtain a college degree, thereby shrinking tuition bills and housing costs. Ask your high school guidance counselor if your district offers these opportunities.

Testing Out

Finally, students can petition to take an exam to prove competency in course material at many colleges. If you feel you've already mastered the content in a particular course, this is a cost-saving avenue to explore. At most schools, there is no charge for attempting to earn credit-by-exam, with a considerable upside if you do succeed. These exams are generally created by individual professors, and therefore are less predictable than a standardized test, such as the CLEP. Nevertheless, if a student is bright and confident in his grasp of the material, why not give it a go? Normally, these exams are no harm, no foul, meaning that if you fail the test, there is no punishment other than having to take the course you were trying to avoid.

Waiting until you enroll in college to begin cutting costs is a huge mistake. You want to max out on AP, IB, and dual enrollment credits during high school. In a few instances, some high-achieving students have even managed to knock off nearly two entire years of college using the tools outlined here. In the time and for the cost it takes a typical undergraduate to earn the bachelor's degree, such a go-getter will be able to complete a master's program. Smart, indeed.

THE IMPORTANCE OF MAJORS

REALITY RULE #7

OLD RULE:	NEW RULE:
It doesn't matter what you major in, as long as you get your degree.	*Majors matter.*

When fewer of us attended college, academic majors were a matter of little consequence. One was nearly as good as another, because the mere fact that a student held a BA or BS degree was enough to set her apart from the masses lacking one. You were a college graduate, after all! That said a lot, back in the day. Unless a student was preparing for a specific subset of careers requiring structured preparation, it made little difference if she had been a history, literature, or political science major.

Ongoing credential inflation over the years, however, has created much keener competition within the ranks of degree holders. Today, majors matter more than ever. A new college graduate does not only have to compete for employment against this year's graduates. She now also has to compete against last year's graduates, many of whom are still unemployed. She must compete against legions of other unemployed adults, with considerable work experience, vying for the few available positions. Many displaced baby boomers, at the ends of their careers, are taking entry-level positions that normally would go to recent college graduates in order to shore up their deflated savings.

EMPLOYERS WILL BE CHOOSIER

Because the diploma alone is not a strong enough discriminating factor in hiring anymore, employers can afford to look more closely at degrees and majors. Employers can and will be more particular about whom they hire during times of economic stress, and they are going to prefer the candidate whose preparation most closely matches the available job. This means that they will scrutinize majors and work experience.

According to the National Center for Education Statistics, the most popular major in America today by a long shot is the business major. Approximately 20 percent of all bachelor's degrees awarded go to business majors. The next most popular choice is a combination of social sciences and history, which accounts for roughly half the number of business majors. The next most popular majors are education, health and clinical sciences, and psychology.

═══COLLEGE BY THE NUMBERS═══

According to the National Center for Education Statistics, in the 2007–2008 school year (the most recent year for which numbers were available), colleges awarded undergraduate degrees in:

- business (335,000)
- social sciences and history (167,000)
- health sciences (111,000)
- education (103,000)

Leading master's degrees included:
- education (176,000)
- business (156,000)

It's a pretty good bet if you major in one of these top fields, you will face a lot of competition from other graduates bearing the same credential. This is basic supply and demand. Of course, health care should see growing demand, as baby boomers age, and education expects large numbers of retirements in coming years, which could make these majors good long-term bets despite their popularity. The point is that students need to do their research and review reliable information to select a college major that will pay off. Wishful thinking is not terribly helpful in a tough job market.

During a down economy, major selection deserves extra attention. Truth be told, the average college student probably spends about as much time deciding upon a major as deciding what to have for dinner from the cafeteria. Often, students make their selections based on little more than a favorite teacher or on one class that they found easy or enjoyable. The decision is typically based more on personal interests than on external market demands or economic forces. According to Nicholas Lore, the author of *Now What? The Young Person's Guide to Choosing the Perfect Career*, the typical major and career selection process goes something like this:

"During your last years of high school, your parents and your guidance counselor ask you to 'start thinking about what you may want to do.' You, having no experience in this sort of thing, may come up with some possible careers, or you may not. The ideas most people come up with at this point are based on almost no evidence and not enough self-knowledge to think of anything suitable. Often their ideas are based on what seems cool at the time. You would be amazed at how many lawyers decide on their careers because of some movie or TV show, which bears no resemblance to the real practice of law. No wonder so many hate their jobs. In college, you find yourself faced with choosing a major without much more clarity than you had in high school. By the time you reach the head of the line you have to decide, so you do."

"FINDING YOURSELF"

Historically, college has been a carefree time when young people were exempt from adult obligations, when they could explore a variety of interests before making a firm decision and commitment to an occupational path. This "moratorium" period described by psychologist James Marcia (see Chapter 2) is growing longer and longer in America, as our lifespan grows and adolescence is extended. One contributing reason for this is the unavailability of jobs, due to the oversupply of older workers.

The problem is that a moratorium is expensive. A few generations ago, most American youth helped to support their families before the age of eighteen. My grandfather left school at the age of twelve to go to work, and only went back to college later in life. Today, such an early end to childhood is unthinkable; we want our children to enjoy a few years after high school before assuming adult responsibilities, but most middle-class American families still expect their child to be employed soon after graduating from college. It is really only the upper classes who can afford to give their children unfettered freedom to pursue interests and majors with complete disregard for potential career implications.

I remember that my own approach to selecting a college major was dictated by the prevailing advice at the time. Harvard informed us repeatedly that it didn't matter what we majored in, because we were going to be liberal arts graduates and the most important thing we would be learning was "how to learn." That sounded good to me, so I flirted with the idea of being a history and literature major, but ultimately settled on English. When my parents asked me what kind of job I expected to get with a degree in English, I responded honestly that I didn't know, but I hoped to be a writer.

The Value of an Ivy League Education—Or Not?

I did expect that having a degree from an elite Ivy League school would counteract whatever limitations my choice of major might have on my post-college employment opportunities, but I was wrong. When senior year rolled around, and the country was mired in a deep recession, I visited the (limited) recruiters who attended Harvard's job fair and found that they were mostly Wall Street firms and various consulting agencies looking for economics majors. I did not find one employer there who was interested in interviewing an English major—not even the advertising agencies.

That lack of demand would have been good information to have during my freshmen and sophomore years. No one bothered to share that with me, and I didn't know to ask what majors would be in demand by the main employers represented at Harvard's job fair. In retrospect, I believe that the advice I was given was more appropriate for a wealthy student who did not have to be concerned with such mundane realities as making a living or paying rent right after college. I suspect that Harvard and my professors really didn't know what advice to offer to middle-class students, other than the standard counsel they were used to giving to every student: Study whatever you like.

Young adulthood is, without a doubt, one of the most stressful times of life. Most parents and students are completely exhausted by the college admissions and financial aid processes, so it's not surprising that selecting a major may seem to be a mere afterthought to overcoming those enormous hurdles. Many parents are also unwilling to limit their child's freedom to consider all the possible majors and so refrain from trying to influence this decision in one direction or another.

According to research by Penn State, up to 80 percent of students entering college admit that they're not certain about what they really want to major in. Even after that, uncertainty remains so strong that nearly half of all college students will switch majors at least once. Switching majors, as I previously remarked, can be a very costly choice, because students may lose valuable credits and dramatically slow down their progress toward graduation.

Ideally, aspiring college students should make their career decision first. The next step is to select the major that will provide the best preparation for the desired career, and then finally select the college that offers the best program in that field. Career–major–college. Most students do the exact reverse—college, then major, and finally career—with disappointing results.

Students and parents often look at college as a place where young people can "find themselves." This is all well and good, but my view is that students without clear career goals can "find themselves" just as easily at an affordable college as at a high-priced one. I would recommend that parents insist on career clarity for college options costing more than $30,000 per year. The greater the level of career clarity, and the brighter the career options in that field, the more you can safely invest in expensive degree programs.

Students should only be going to the highest-priced colleges if they are pursuing the highest-paying careers. This is a fair and reasonable guideline to set.

Sit down and calculate starting salaries (check *www.salary .com*) and figure out how long it would take to pay back the loans on a high-priced degree. This is the only way to make realistic choices. Furthermore, if it really doesn't matter what you major in—as many counselors, professors, and college administrators confidently assert—then why *not* major in something in demand? You might as well.

It is easier to sail with the wind than against it, and the reality is that some majors do pay more and are in much higher demand. (The National Association of Colleges and Employers' most recent survey of college graduates found that preprofessional majors received higher salary offers than liberal arts and sciences majors and that majors that boast technical skills earned the highest offer rates.) To choose a college major successfully, students will need to test the direction of the wind and plan accordingly. This means finding out where labor force demand is likely to be highest when they graduate and preparing for fields in those areas, when possible. As Shakespeare wisely advised, "There is a tide in the affairs of men which, taken at the flood, leads on to fortune." Whenever possible, don't fight the tide.

Aligning Your Interests

But what about my interests and talents, you might ask? Shouldn't that determine what I'll major in? I would answer that you won't have much time to indulge in them if you can't support yourself or make a decent living after college. Ideally, you will be able to find a way to combine these to find an ideal career path. To quote another sage ancient, Aristotle, "Where your talents and the world's needs cross, there lies your vocation." The problem that I often see when counseling young people about careers is a lack of understanding of what the world's needs are.

The message delivered to college students always seems to be that one major is as good as any other. This may be true in some intellectual respects, but it is not true for employers. In a tough job market, employers can afford to be discerning, and they will be. They will select graduates with majors closely tied to their field of enterprise. If they don't need to look further than that to find suitable candidates, they won't.

According to Dan Bernardo of Factoidz, within ten years, 70 percent of college graduates will not be working in a field related to their major. The key challenge for today's young people, in my view, is getting an initial job offer. Majors certainly become much less important over the years as an employee proves herself on the job and advances, but the major can be instrumental in landing that first, crucial entry-level position and in convincing an employer to take a chance on you as an unknown entity.

In times of plenty, it might not matter much what a student majors in, but in times of economic scarcity and job contraction, the smart move is to choose majors that are going to be in demand in the short-term. I believe that the idealistic advice to "major in whatever you want" might realistically apply only to the top segment of wealthiest Americans with no financial constraints. I suspect that this impractical advice persists because it was functional enough back when most college students were from the privileged upper classes with connections and the financial means to pursue employment as an avocation. We want to believe that by sending our children to college, they will enjoy those same privileges. This is simply not the case for the majority of current college students. This advice also works reasonably well when the economy is roaring and entry-level employment opportunities are plentiful. This is also not currently the case.

The fact that this advice is still being offered in an environment when graduates are facing one of the highest unemployment rates in American history is irresponsible. It's a lovely thought, but it does not serve most students well, and students are unlikely to be happy if their choice of major leads to poverty or non-college-level employment. For those who need to work for a living, college majors will continue to matter until such time as a labor shortage develops.

The Benefit of Job Fairs

One of the best pieces of advice I can offer to an undeclared college student is to start attending job fairs immediately—even if you are still in high school. You don't have to plan on getting a job right then and there. Go as an observer: Walk around, and pay attention to which employers are attending. Listen to what they have to say and ask them, What types of college majors do you hire at your organization? If you're thinking about selecting a particular major, ask the employer how she would feel about an applicant with that academic background. Get your information straight from the source.

Without a career plan, students risk selecting a major carelessly and haphazardly, and winding up with a degree in a field in low or no demand. Currently, the guidance college students receive on major selection tends to encourage any choice at all. This is very egalitarian, but it's not realistic, nor is it reflective of current economic conditions and differing job outlooks. Colleges often hold Majors Fairs where students can walk from table to table and speak to students or professors representing the different majors available on campus. Naturally, each of these representatives will tell you how wonderful their field is. In my opinion, Majors Fairs ought to be aligned with Job Fairs, in order to ascertain which majors are most likely to position students for long-term success.

Parents, I'm not suggesting that you should try to talk your children out of majors on which they have their hearts set in favor of ones that seems more employment-worthy. Enthusiasm and passion are probably the key ingredients for success in life, and a student with a high level of commitment and talent in a low-demand field can still find success, despite considerable odds. It may be an uphill battle, however. For the overwhelming majority of students who are vague on what they want to major in, a directive approach geared to the emerging job market is probably best.

I believe that many aspects of college planning are backward. For instance, the college admissions deadlines precede the financial aid process, so at the point students are completing applications to schools they don't know whether or not they can realistically afford to attend. Likewise, the career-planning calendar is also reversed, with most students selecting colleges and majors before they decide on their career path. High school seniors have to pick a college, so that decision takes priority over all others. It's such a time-consuming process, that it tends to distract attention from everything else. College sophomores need to declare a major, so that decision comes next. Finally, college seniors need to find jobs, so that is when most undergraduates will finally turn their attention to the work world. At this point, many will find that they are unprepared for a smooth entry.

QUESTIONS FOR A PROSPECTIVE MAJOR

Here are some career-oriented questions parents and students should ask about each potential college major:

- **Will students have access to paid internships in this major? (This is generally a very strong indication of how in-demand different majors are. Employers will offer paid internships to students studying fields in high demand, while they will expect students in low-demand fields with plentiful applicants to labor for free.)**

- **How many of your graduates had job offers in the field by graduation last year?**

■ **What was the starting pay for hired graduates?**

■ **How many graduates are working in fields related to this major ten years later?**

■ **Do you conduct satisfaction surveys of alumni in this major? If so, do you have the results?**

■ **Which employers send recruiters annually to hire students in this major?**

■ **What specific parameters do these employers place on the students they will interview? Do they expect a certain GPA, for example?**

I suggest directing these questions both to professors or administrators within academic departments and also to the campus career center. If professors and career counselors are unwilling or unable to answer these questions, then you must judge accordingly before investing in the degree programs they are offering.

When Do You Want to Work?

Families should also consider this question before selecting a major: How soon after graduation does the student need to start working? We all operate under legitimate economic constraints and our funds are not limitless. Obviously, students with trust funds or a family's financial backing can afford to delay their entry to the paid workforce longer than those with no financial cushion. Families from the upper classes may be able and willing to allow a child to delay full assumption of adult responsibilities post-college.

Parents, you need to be honest about when you expect your child to be off the family payroll. The sooner you need your graduate to be self-sustaining, the more assertive you should be about encouraging him to seek an employment-friendly major. Students, you should think about when you want or need to start earning money to support yourself and be out on your own. Make a realistic evaluation of how much money you'll need in order to be independent of your parents.

WHAT TIME IS IT?

Sociologists sometimes refer to the age at which we expect a person to reach certain milestones as the *social clock*. There is a class element to this theory; the lower classes generally expect their children to reach important milestones, such as finishing school, much sooner than the upper classes do. Simply put, they need their children to find jobs because they can't afford to support them any longer.

It might help to point out that, while majors do matter, the selection of a major is not an all-determining choice. At most liberal arts schools, there will still be plenty of elective opportunities for pursuing other interests that offer a lower likelihood of gainful employment. Also, many people eventually shift from their entry-level positions to other lines of work. The hardest job to get is usually the first full-time one, and this is where the college major can play its most important role. After that point, experience, professional connections, and recommendations will help to pave the way to future opportunities.

Differentiate Yourself

Here are two more important questions students should be able to answer about each possible major:

1. **How will you set yourself apart with this major?**

2. **What will you be able to do, when you are finished, that employers or customers will be willing to pay for?**

If you cannot answer these questions, or can only answer them vaguely, then it's time to begin collecting more definitive information about the majors you're considering. These questions will help both parents and students find out about actual career prospects in a potential field; then you must supplement this knowledge with facts and research. *A parent's role is not to judge or control a student's choice.* Rather you should serve as a consultant and concerned reality checker, providing factual information and practical assistance. And, who knows? Your child may surprise you with good answers that will allay your concerns.

The truth is, too many college students and their parents make major decisions the same way they select a college: for fairly superficial and emotional reasons. Many will choose the path of least resistance and select the major that seems easiest. These are not selection criteria likely to lead to lasting success or to provide an edge in a competitive job market. To help a student prepare for success today, both of you are going to have to do better than that.

This is hard advice to follow, but it is worth reiterating: Students should choose their career *first, then* select the major which leads to that career, and *finally* decide upon a college with an outstanding major program in the desired field. Instead, most families get this completely backward. They postpone career decisions, focus first on finding a college that looks nice, attend for a few years, select a major that seems interesting, and then senior year start looking around for places to send resumes and job applications. Most college students will go down this path, with predictably poor results. To separate one's results from the rest of the pack and overcome distressing employment odds, smart students must pursue college attendance with a different, more effective strategy from the one that has failed for so many.

STILL UNDECIDED

What if a student is already in college and still undecided about her major? In that case, I advise you to consider the full range of interests and aptitudes but to err on the side of choosing a higher-paying major over a lower-paying one. One nice aspect of a typical liberal arts degree is that it allows a student the flexibility to take elective courses in a number of interesting areas. A student who chooses to major in accounting for career purposes can still enjoy courses in archaeology or philosophy. He can even minor in one of those fields, but he would be smart to select a major that pays a living wage.

═COLLEGE BY THE NUMBERS═

Which majors pay best? According to *www.payscale*

.com most of the highest-paying college majors are

in engineering, with petroleum engineering lead-

ing the list. Beyond engineering, other high-paying

majors (above $50,000 to start) include economics,

computer science, and industrial engineering. Some

of the worst paying college majors include drama,

fine arts, hospitality and tourism, music, theology,

and social work.

No, it's not fair to a student with a flair for the

arts, but this is economic reality and every college-

bound student must be concerned about financial

survival in tough times.

The same basic advice goes for competing passions. If a
student loves music and math, encourage her to pursue math
as the major with an extracurricular focus or minor in music.
Likewise, if you love painting and drawing, you can always pursue these interests in elective courses or as hobbies or sidelines
in adulthood as long as you have the ability to support yourself.
These choices do not have to be mutually exclusive.

Passion or Career?

Some people say, "Do what you love and you will never have to work a day in your life." This advice sounds good to an aspiring artist, but it is hard to love what you do when your home is being foreclosed on and you can't afford health insurance. Others believe, "The fastest way to destroy your passion for something is to make a career out of it." How do we balance between these competing views? Sometimes, it makes sense to separate our vocations and avocations.

Remember, too, that passions don't necessary have to be lost in the struggle to earn a living. Your career is only one aspect of a full life. One way of looking at the compromises we sometimes have to make is that high-paying jobs often *liberate* us to follow our passions, whereas low-paying ones can consume all our waking hours and destroy our freedom and choices.

Here's another rule of thumb that can't lose: When you have to choose between different career and major possibilities, simply choose the one that pays the most per hour. That way, you will have more hours available to pursue your other interests, because you will be able to support yourself in fewer hours. It is a very lifestyle-enhancing way to think.

CHEAT SHEET

COLLEGE SELECTION QUESTIONNAIRE

Here are college selection criteria, for parents and students, in descending order of importance:

1. CAREER

Will it take you where you need to go? ------------------------------

----

How are the professors in the intended major? ----------------------

----

Where do graduates find jobs? (Talk to the career center and department chair.)

----

2. COST

Will they give you need-based or merit aid? ------------------------

What return on this investment can you expect? ---------------------

----

Does it pass the sleep test? (Will you be able to sleep at night with this college choice or be up worried about bills and loans?)

----

3. CULTURE

Will you make friends there? --------------------------------------

After eating in the cafeteria and seeing the cars in the student parking lot, do you feel like you/your student would fit in?

Is there a strong political bent on campus? (Check the student newspaper and the flyers posted on kiosks.) Is that okay with you?

----

4. CLIMATE

Will the location help with finding contacts in the workforce?

Is it in the region of the country you want? ------------------------

Can you find the activities you like at the school and in the surrounding area?

PART II

PAYING FOR COLLEGE WITHOUT GOING BROKE

Caveat emptor

CHAPTER 5

EVALUATING THE FINANCIAL INVESTMENT

ollege costs are spinning out of control, taking family finances with them. These days, it seems as if the middle class is already teetering on the economic brink, and then college comes along to push us over the edge of insolvency. The average family used to be able to count on college as a net gain to the family's wealth, contributing far more than it cost. As the number of individuals attending college grows, it is likely that the return to each individual attendee will shrink, following the basic laws of supply and demand in the economic marketplace. Presumably, the greater the supply of college graduates, the lower the price to hire each one. Couple that trend with dramatically higher tuition costs, and it is clear that "college at any cost" is no longer a viable strategy for every American family.

Most families, except those with unlimited finances, are going to have to be more restrained in their college expenditures until such time that the current oversupply of college graduates is absorbed by the workforce and the demand for college degrees reestablishes itself. In the meantime, you must exercise financial prudence when making college plans to ensure that the investment pays off.

REALITY RULE #8

OLD RULE:	NEW RULE:
A college degree ensures financial security.	*College can be a risky financial investment; hedge your bets.*

Most of us have grown up with the comforting notion that a college degree will always pay off and that it is always worth it, no matter the price. Many people also believe that, while a college degree may not guarantee riches, it can at least be counted on to provide financial security. Traditionally, it's been seen as one of the safest economic bets around. Because of these firm convictions, families routinely tap into significant portions of their lifetime savings—even to the point of re-mortgaging their homes, in many cases—to bankroll the college educations of their children. Colleges and the financial aid system expect and, in fact, demand, these dramatic expenditures, but they are increasingly difficult to justify in light of current documented rates of return on bachelor's degrees.

COLLEGE BY THE NUMBERS

Today nearly 20 percent of the unemployed in the United States have college degrees while less than half of all college graduates under age twenty-five are working in jobs that require them. According to the Bureau of Labor Statistics, there are currently over 482,000 customer service representatives with college degrees, along with 317,000 waiters and waitresses. There are also over 80,000 bartenders and 18,000 parking lot attendants—part of a total of 17 million Americans with college degrees working at jobs that do not require college-level skills. It is clear that in today's circumstances, students are going to need more than just a college diploma to escape the scary reality embodied by those unsettling statistics. Therefore, putting a family's entire nest egg on the line to finance a sheepskin may actually turn out to be an expensive gamble rather than a safe bet.

$

IS COLLEGE THE BEST INVESTMENT?

With these facts in mind, before we discuss how to realistically evaluate and control the costs of a college education, it's worth asking the seemingly unaskable question: Is a college education the best investment of your family's money?

There are many reasons to send a child to college, but one thing is clear: It can no longer always be considered to be a smart financial move; now you must approach it with caution, circumspection, and fiscal restraint. There is no doubt that many colleges are overpriced right now and that the financial returns are increasingly iffy. For a growing number of families, college will turn out to be a bad investment. In this precarious economy, there are actually several other financial ventures that are now beginning to look more appealing.

Imagine that an extremely frugal family has saved $200,000 for college. I realize that this number is unrealistic for most families, but let's use it for the sake of argument. Would it make more sense to spend that money on four years of college, or to invest it differently?

Real Estate

What if this family decided to use the money to purchase a home for the child, instead of paying for college? This would certainly be going against the grain, but the most successful investors have always acted contrary to majority opinion.

Real estate values have plunged in recent years, while college tuitions have skyrocketed. In the mid-1980s when I attended college, four years at Harvard cost a total of about $60,000. That was a large amount of money in those days, but still not enough to buy an average house. The average home price in 1986 was $92,000—about $30,000 more. Most of us still have the idea in our heads that a college education should easily cost less than a house.

Flash forward to today. The price of the average home now is $192,000 and falling like a rock, while that same Harvard education now costs over $210,000. The average home now costs $20,000 *less* than the same college degree.

It's quite possible that your family's savings, invested in a home, could turn out to have a better rate of return than if you spent it on tuition. Such a purchase could conceivably spare your son or daughter sixty years' worth of mortgage interest or rent payments. Consider the lifetime yield on that investment! Can a college degree provide a return like that?

For a young adult, home ownership would eliminate the desperate imperative to find a job (any job!) just to cover the bills (especially the student loan payment), since the biggest cost of modern life—housing—would be covered for life. This would provide substantial breathing room and financial security. You or your offspring could always sell the house and pocket the proceeds, something you cannot do with a college education.

If mortgage interest rates and property values rise, as they certainly will eventually, the returns on this investment could be even higher. A student who owned his own home, free and clear, could work for a few years, gain experience, explore various career options, and ultimately pay his own college tuition out of his earned income, rather than using debt as the primary funding method.

Entrepreneurship

What about taking that $200,000 and investing it in a business rather than in a college education? A young adult who owns his own business would not have to rely on strangers in human resource departments to pick his resume out of a stack of thousands to determine his opportunities in life. He could steer his own ship, own his own job, and never be unemployed. This option ought to be considered as well, taking into consideration the child's abilities, preferences, and entrepreneurial spirit.

Even the rocky stock market might possibly offer better returns than an investment in higher education. Over the past thirty years, the S&P 500 Index averaged about 11 percent a year. Only 88 colleges out of 554 schools analyzed in a recent PayScale "Return on Investment" study offered a better return on investment to their students than the S&P. You can find more details on this study, including the schools delivering the best rates of return, here: *www.payscale.com/education/average-cost-for-college-ROI*. Everywhere else, this study implies, students would have been financially better off if they had taken the money they spent on their college educations, invested it in the stock market, and never set foot inside a classroom. Ouch.

My point is not to discourage you from higher education, but to be sure that you understand that there are competing options to consider and that the college education you select must justify its costs. College has been oversold as a rock-solid financial investment. There is no guarantee of a job after degree completion. There is also no guarantee of a degree at all, should a student be unmotivated and academically disinterested.

The only thing that *is* guaranteed is that tuition bills must be paid and student loans will have to be repaid. The lenders will have their money, no matter what. The choice of paying for college always has to be weighed against alternative uses of that money and a realistic appraisal of the actual financial returns that can be expected.

CONTROLLING THE COSTS

Let's assume that you and your family have discussed the alternatives I've presented above and have decided to go ahead with plans to send your son or daughter to college. Here are steps you must take to dramatically reduce the costs of obtaining a bachelor's degree, helping to increase the return on the investment.

REALITY RULE #9

OLD RULE:	NEW RULE:
Go to the best school that you can get into.	*Go where the deal is best.*

Counselors and advisers constantly exhort high school students to go to the best college they can get into. This is especially true of strong students at the top of their classes. Our culture, through the media, educational institutions, and so on, encourages families to allow high school students complete freedom to choose their dream schools. Once they make their choices, the conventional wisdom goes, parents can figure out how to pay for the selections. Of course, the implicit hope of most families is that financial aid is going to magically swoop in to somehow make the college affordable and keep the family financially whole.

If this is your line of thinking, then I have a question for you: Did you allow your child to decide what home you purchased and the monthly mortgage you assumed? Of course not. Children don't understand anything about mortgages, property taxes, maintenance costs, utilities, or your income level. Well, unfortunately, college today is becoming a mortgage-sized expenditure.

Here are two important points to keep in mind: First, the average high school senior understands little about personal finances. Second, as the Nobel Laureate economist Milton Friedman tells us, "very few people spend other people's money as carefully as they spend their own." This is true at the micro-individual level, and it is true at the macro-societal level. We need merely look at our government's growing debt problem to see that elected officials are extremely generous with funds not coming from their own pockets. Likewise, most adolescents, given free rein, will choose the most luxurious college option with no concern for the costs involved. Without reasonable guidance and constraints, the entire family is liable to wind up in financial jeopardy given today's high tuition prices.

REINING IN THE MONEY

It is up to parents to put the brakes on unnecessary and exorbitant college expenditures, which means having a hard conversation about cost limitations early on in the selection process. No, it won't be fun, but it is fair, it is responsible, and it is increasingly necessary. Without this talk, a student is liable to end up with a bad case of buyer's remorse, much like Kelli Space, with her mind-boggling $200,000 financial obligation for her bachelor's degree in sociology. Her monthly payments of nearly $900 are due to double soon. Asked by a *Boston Herald* blogger if she wishes she had chosen a less expensive school, Space says:

> "*I absolutely look back and regret attending such an expensive school. I could have even gone the community-school-for-two-years-and-transfer route, but it hadn't crossed my mind as an option. I was spoiled in that I thought I deserved*

*to attend the best school that granted me admission.
Clearly, not the best overall school of thought."*

On her website, where she now solicits donations to help her pay back her debt obligation, Space says: "I was 18 and the first person in my family . . . to attend college. Therefore, not only was excitement consuming me, but my parents didn't exactly know how college would or wouldn't affect my salary in the future . . . They heard—as much as I did—that cost of tuition should never keep you from attending a great school. So we made the mistake of following such romantic advice."

The excitement of the prospect of college and the natural inclination of parents not to disappoint their children often combine to fuel irrational monetary decisions for the college-bound. Don't make that mistake in your family. Young high school graduates like Kelli deserve to be protected from making an enormous, yet understandable, financial mistake right out of the starting gate of life.

I have to wonder how any lender was willing to loan her this much money, and I couldn't help noticing that her college expenses included a semester spent abroad in Ireland. A trip to Ireland is hardly a necessity for a student studying sociology, which is, incidentally, one of the lowest-paying college majors. Young Kelli is in for decades of hurt, now that her four short years of college are behind her. I bet she wishes she and her parents had discussed financial limitations before she enrolled.

It is understandable and commendable that parents want to help finance their child's college dreams, but it's also crucial not to lose our heads. Emotion rules and rationality often flies out the window when families discuss college, and the vague mysteries of the financial aid process help to make delusions possible. You are not doing a student any favors if you set him or her up for the kind of financial pain facing Kelli Space. Wouldn't you rather select an affordable college education, which will likely provide an equally firm career platform, and a debt-free start to adulthood?

The better informed that parents are about the financial realities of college and the amount of aid to expect, the more realistic these necessary economic discussions will be. For most families, however, the final verdict on cost will not arrive from financial aid offices until spring of senior year, so—and this is vitally important—wait until then to make your final college decisions. To be financially responsible, all families (except those for whom money is no object) should keep their options open until they've have had the opportunity to compare financial aid packages.

HIGHER TUITION, BETTER RESULTS?

Despite the absence of credible evidence, there seems to be a tendency to associate higher tuition costs with a higher quality of education. It even appears that some schools may be keeping their tuition artificially high merely to convey the *impression* of value and exclusivity, and to avoid the perception that they are cheaper, and therefore less desirable, than their competitors. For instance, an article entitled "The Prestige Racket" which appeared in *Washington Monthly* describes

George Washington University's drive to join the elite schools with top college rankings. GWU former president Stephen Joel Trachtenberg believed that a higher tuition price would elevate the stature of his school and that families would pay a premium for the perceived status that went along with it. You could call it the Chivas Regal effect. He suspected that students unable to gain admission to the nation's most selective colleges would flock to one that offered a matching price tag as an indicator of exclusivity. Trachtenberg even argued that, "You can get a Timex or a Casio for $65 or you can get a Rolex or a Patek Philippe for $10,000. It's the same thing."

Do not fall for the mistaken notion that you have to pay a bundle or mortgage your home for a premium-priced college education or your child's life chances will be dashed. It is simply not true, despite all the peer pressure and media hype conspiring to fuel your anxiety over college admissions. The real value of an education always comes from the effort expended by the student, not from the tuition price tag.

I will share some strategies for getting a realistic estimate of the amount of financial aid you can expect, which will help keep you from unnecessarily eliminating higher-priced schools that might actually turn out to be within economic reach. This can reduce some of the guesswork involved.

BREAKING DOWN COLLEGE COSTS

One good tactic for looking at college costs is figuring out exactly what the different options will mean to both the student and the parents. When you break the numbers down into what the different options will mean for everyone, the information will have a far greater impact, since college costs are bundled in such enormous terms that even most adults can barely wrap their heads around them.

For instance, if a student selects the most expensive college alternative, he may need to work every summer and sell his car. He also might not be able to afford study abroad—an expensive add-on that an increasing number of college students seem to feel is absolutely necessary. (Incidentally, are you aware that studies have shown that students studying abroad tend to drink much more heavily than students remaining on campus? Do you really want to pay extra for that?) He may even have to move back into his old bedroom after college to afford to pay back the student loans, as an increasing number of graduates are discovering.

On the other hand, if he chooses the less expensive alternative (perhaps a public university or a merit aid offer at a less prestigious school), then he may be able to travel instead of working during the summer, keep his car, and have a much more affordable post-college budget. Concrete terms like these are more likely to make clear the real impact of the college financial burden on the family and will force everyone to seriously consider the full range of postsecondary options.

═══COLLEGE BY THE NUMBERS═══

If you're afraid that the less expensive college alternative might somehow doom your child's life chances, consider this: According to People Capital, an organization that tracks earning potential, an average graduate of an expensive, high-debt private college such as George Washington University will have about the same lifetime earning potential coming out of a much more affordable public university. In other words, the payoff for the *less* expensive school is higher.

─────────────────$─────────────────

One infuriating problem, in my view, is that colleges treat students as adults for all purposes *except* the most burdensome one: paying the bills. For instance, if parents want to see a student's college grades or communicate with his professors, they are out of luck. Because of the Family Educational Rights and Privacy Act (FERPA), your college student is considered an adult for educational purposes, and all formal communication from the college must go through him. What about the bills, you may rightly wonder? Well, you can have those. This seems like a case of selective adulthood.

As proud recipients of all those future tuition bills, parents should feel empowered to confidently assert authority in this matter. Let the deliberations commence, investigate all the options, but maintain financial veto power over outcomes that place your family's, or your student's, economic future at risk.

MINIMIZE COST, MAXIMIZE GAIN

To economically survive in today's world, families may need to withhold some of their limited funds to ensure that there will be enough left over after college to provide whatever additional assistance a student will require post-graduation. Realistically, this may mean choosing less expensive bachelor's degree options, such as public colleges or community college transfer programs. Like any other expensive endeavor, you should weigh the costs against the potential yield and consider other possible uses of that money. You always have to measure the level of any investment against a rational appraisal of the realistic rate of return that you can expect.

To hedge your college bets, then, you need to minimize your costs while maximizing your gains. Obviously, the less money you place on the table, the lower your risk. Affordable colleges decrease the amount of your "skin in the game," so every student ought to consider lower-priced institutions, unless financial aid will be chipping in to help cover your college costs. Minimizing costs also involves proactively seeking as much aid as possible.

There are many ways of maximizing gains, such as choosing high-paying majors, studying the workforce to select in-demand fields, and seeking programs with demonstrated records of employing graduates. As the college affordability crisis continues to unfold, you can expect to see more calls for higher education institutions to disclose the success rates of graduates, so that consumers can make more informed choices about where to invest their limited funds.

Diversify!

Finally, one of the best ways of hedging bets has always been to diversify. This means considering the possibility of investing a certain proportion of money in a student's undergraduate degree costs, but limiting the amount you are willing to spend on this one aspect of preparing a child for adulthood. If, for example, your student attends a less expensive college, then you may be able to reserve enough assets to afford to help him purchase a foreclosed property, start a business, or attend graduate school later—investments that might possibly offer higher financial returns in the short or long run. This might turn out to be considerably wiser than betting all of your accumulated assets on an expensive bachelor's degree.

MAXIMIZING YOUR FINANCIAL AID

REALITY RULE #10

OLD RULE:	NEW RULE:
A college degree is always a good investment at any price.	*Never pay the asking price; hold out for a better deal.*

rior generations, who enjoyed far lower tuition costs, received good returns on their college investments. This is one reason why they are quick to encourage future generations to attend. Of course, these prior generations also benefited from decades of appreciating home prices. Over the years, they likewise passed along the traditional advice that buying a home is always a good investment. This belief held sway in spite of growing evidence, during the first decade of the 2000s, to the contrary, as home prices rose far beyond rental prices in many regions of the country. Simple common sense should have told potential buyers that they would have been better off renting than buying when mortgages reached questionable highs, but instead the upward spiral in prices caused a buying frenzy. Home prices defied gravity for a while, until they finally crashed back down to earth. The results of following that outdated real estate advice, at the wrong time in history, have been devastating to many people and to the economy at large.

In many ways, the college bubble is already bursting:

- **For graduates who cannot find jobs worthy of their level of higher education**

- **For parents who watch in dismay as their graduates move back home unable to find work**

- **For students with loans to repay who do not have the means to repay them**

This last group is the one that is going to cause wider effects in the overall economy, as the burden of federal loan defaults falls, predictably, once again on the shoulders of the American taxpayer, who unwittingly backed them.

COLLEGE EDUCATION FOR EVERYONE?

Ever since the GI Bill paved the way for increased access to higher education post–World War II, college has expanded to ever-widening segments of the population until now a majority of high school students attend. All of them, presumably, expect to earn above-average incomes after they graduate, even though this clearly defies mathematical possibilities. Not too long ago, President Obama even asked *every* American to commit to post-secondary education, stating that, "We expect all our children not only to graduate from high school but to graduate from college and get a good-paying job."

Really? All of them? This feel-good assertion from the banks of Lake Woebegon (where, as author Garrison Keillor claims, "all children are above average") may sound nice, but this is a potentially perilous path. If everyone had a college degree, the result could very well be universal credential inflation and a higher cost of entry and age to the workforce.

Whether college will continue to pay off for future generations remains to be seen, but currently, many college graduates are not seeing impressive returns on their investment in higher education and the labor force has been unable to absorb the growing number of graduates. It appears that there is an upper limit to the number of students who can attend college without devaluing the commodity itself.

A college education cannot possibly be a never-ending source of prosperity for an unlimited number of students, regardless of their levels of ambition or native intelligence, especially since they are being asked to go into so much debt to acquire it. In the same way, there's an upper limit to the number of people who can trade and flip a house and receive more than they paid for it. Eventually, the economy simply runs out of more buyers, and then the precarious game collapses.

College can actually be a terrible investment for some students. Just ask any of the unemployed graduates from the last few years, many of whom are still residing in their childhood bedrooms or parents' basements, waiting for their opportunities to join the workforce at the college level. They are likely to be waiting a very long time unless they acquire some marketable job skills. Former British Prime Minister Gordon Brown recently warned that the world is facing a growing youth unemployment problem of "epidemic proportions." Likewise, Harvard's Graduate School of Education reports that, "The percentages of teens and young adults who are working are now at the lowest levels recorded since the end of the 1930s Depression." This is hardly an economic environment supporting such unwarranted optimism or dramatic expenditures on college.

For all these reasons, we need to make sure, when we've made the decision for college, that we use the best possible strategies to keep costs down and maximize the return on our investment.

EXPECT A DISCOUNT

Thrifty people often abide by the motto to "never pay retail." If you've ever worked in retail, you know that the amount of markup can easily be double or triple the wholesale cost of a product. If you wait—or sometimes if you just ask—you can receive a substantial discount. There is no reason why you should not carry this same mentality to your college planning, especially since the commodity of higher education is currently overpriced relative to the returns you can expect. In fact, one new national survey indicates that colleges are increasingly aware of rising concerns from families about tuition and affordability and a significant number of them are increasing their discount rate (the percentage off the sticker price that students actually pay) in response. (See *www.insidehighered.com/news/survey/admissions2011.*)

Many people do in fact receive considerable discounts on their college tuition, and you should set this as your base expectation. In fact, it is possible for a group of students in the same exact college to sit in the same classroom, receiving the same instruction, while they are all paying wildly different fees.

When another student pays half, a third, or a quarter of the amount your family is charged to attend a certain school, is your child's education going to be worth double or triple what the discounted student's degree is worth? Of course not. This realization is similar to the sickening feeling you get when you board a plane with your ticket and glance over at the fellow seated next to you and realize that he paid a fraction of the amount you did to reach the same destination. It leaves you feeling rather foolish and wishing you had insisted on getting a better deal for yourself. It can almost be enough to ruin your trip.

═══COLLEGE BY THE NUMBERS═══

Consider this alarming fact: If you send your child to a private college that costs $50,000 annually, you are looking at paying $1,000 a week for the next four years. Can you think of anything else that costs $1,000 a week? Perhaps the only things with comparable costs are resort vacations or cruises. Well, you are definitely going to need some discounts on this high-priced, four-year-long voyage.

═══════════════**$**═══════════════

The Need to Negotiate

The wild variation in college pricing merely intensifies the need to negotiate discounts. If the college says you will receive none, you ought to seriously consider attending elsewhere, where you are offered more competitive pricing. I believe that every student, no matter how wealthy, can qualify for a discount at a college somewhere, even if it's not your first-choice school.

Because there is no standard price that everyone pays to attend college, you have to join in the bargaining process. If you have a high income, you will have less negotiating power due to the need-based financial aid system, but there are still many options available to you. The most important of these is your prerogative to take your business elsewhere. One positive result of rising college prices is the fact that good students from the underaided middle and upper middle classes are increasingly showing up on public college campuses. This makes these schools increasingly desirable, as their student bodies improve in caliber. This trend is being assisted by the growing numbers of high-quality honors colleges within public universities. These selective programs-within-a-college often come with substantial merit scholarship awards, making them a compelling alternative to a private college that is unwilling to discount its high price. Public universities are offering these programs specifically to try to entice high-achieving students away from "big name" colleges, so why not check out what they have to offer if you qualify? You qualify by virtue of your grades and SAT scores. Sometimes, you have to apply to them separately, with an additional essay requirement—it varies by school.

Middle-class-flight also intensifies the class stratification that is already taking place at pricey private schools, making them less diverse economically, and, in my opinion, less educationally and socially desirable.

THE WEALTHY EDGE

It is not really a secret, anymore, that wealthy, full-pay families often receive an edge in college admissions. Students from families who indicate they will not be applying for any financial aid do receive preferential reviews in admissions at many selective colleges, who look to them to help balance the institution's bottom line. *Inside Higher Ed* recently conducted an annual survey of college admissions directors that indicated a growing interest in these "full-pay" students. Many colleges and universities admit that recruiting more wealthy students is a key goal for their institutions; the interest in these affluent students is so strong that 10 percent of four-year colleges report that the full-pay students they are admitting have lower grades and test scores than do other admitted applicants.

The more students and families refuse unaffordable "deals" at expensive colleges, the sooner these schools will have to make substantive adjustments in their pricing. One of the most discouraging factors I see playing out on the higher education front is that we seem to be returning to an overtly class-based college system, in which the rich have opportunities and advantages that others cannot afford—in other words, an aristocracy.

If a private college does not advertise that it is "need blind," it's safe to assume that the school is "need aware," that when money talks they will listen. Such preferential admissions diminish the validity of the degree and entrench privilege rather than serving as a true indicator of ability or accomplishment. So much for the idea of meritocracy in America! This is yet another reason you should be unimpressed with elite, high-priced degrees and take a closer look at more reasonably priced alternatives.

Fortunately, nearly everyone can receive a discount on college tuition somewhere. With this in mind, *resolve not to pay full price anywhere.* Either you will receive a scholarship, qualify for financial aid, or attend an institution with affordable tuition, but families should adamantly refuse to pay sky-high prices, particularly if you are considering going into debt to do so.

CREATING YOUR OWN DISCOUNTS

Of course, you can always create your own tuition discounts by finding creative or tried-and-true strategies for shaving costs. For instance, a student could spend the first two years at a community college and then transfer—a process that is becoming easier as more and more students switch out of unaffordable expensive schools, creating open spaces. I like to think of this as "awarding yourself a scholarship."

I once spoke to a professor who serves as a foreign language adjunct at several nearby colleges, ranging from the local community college to the regional public university and the elite private college downtown. She shook her head and admitted, "You can take my introductory class for $50 a credit at the community college, a few hundred dollars a credit at the public university, or a few thousand dollars a credit at the private college. Either way, you get me. Same instructor, same course. Your choice." A student could also elect to live at home for the first two years of college, saving the family a tidy sum on room and board.

Honestly, I'm not even sure schools costing more than $50,000 a year really expect families to pay the fees they are charging, but they'll take it if they can get it. So far, enough families seem willing to pay, or to assume debt, to allow schools to continue to keep their prices so high.

Higher education journalist Lynn O'Shaughnessy has reported that New York University, which is known for having high prices and offering limited aid packages, recently called more than 1,800 families of admitted students to advise them to consider whether the cost of attending NYU would be beyond their means. Even some insiders, apparently, are willing to admit that costs have spiraled out of control to the point where they are damaging families. When more families take this advice and walk away rather than trying to meet outrageous college costs with unsustainable debt, colleges will finally be forced to adjust their prices to reasonable levels.

An important caveat: The advice "expect a discount" generally will not work at public universities, which already offer discounted, nonretail prices. The discount at these schools is built into their lower prices. These are the go-to schools for families unable to negotiate discounted pricing at more expensive colleges.

WHEN IT'S JUST NOT WORTH IT

One client of mine was having a very difficult time negotiating with a very expensive college that has a reputation for offering poor financial aid packages. Her son's heart was set on attending, despite all advice from his parents. Finally, one of the financial aid representatives candidly informed this mother that attending their school, at the price her family would be charged, was "not worth it." He told her that when her son enrolled the amount of of loans would grow each year, until it would reach the point where the family simply couldn't afford to pay their cost anymore. Then, they would look into transferring her son to a less expensive school.

At that point, the representative said, they would discover that many of the courses the student had already taken would not transfer, and he would be forced into taking far more credits than necessary in order to finally receive his diploma from a less prestigious school.

My client was utterly astonished and offended at the representative's frankness, but I assured her that this message was a gift. This aid officer was telling her to walk away, although she didn't want to hear it.

127

CHAPTER 6: Maximizing Your Financial Aid

WORK TO PAY TUITION?

What about the idea of working your way through school? Once upon a time, ambitious students were able to work part-time jobs to fund their own tuition bills and relieve their families of much of the burden of funding their college educations. What a quaint notion. Those days are long gone. In 1950, the annual tuition price at Harvard was a mere $600. The minimum wage, at the time, was 75 cents. Therefore, a student earning minimum wage at the time could have earned enough to pay for his own Harvard education in 800 hours—about twenty weeks of full-time employment. It certainly wouldn't have been easy, but it would be doable over the course of a three-month summer vacation with some extra hours picked up during the school year.

Flash forward to the 1980s, when I attended college. At that time, Harvard's tuition price was about $9,000 per year and the minimum wage was $3.35 an hour. Simple division tells us that at that point it would have taken a whopping 2,686 hours to earn that much money: That's 67 weeks of full-time work to pay one year's tuition. In case you're confused at this point, let me remind you that there are only 52 weeks in a year. Throw in room and board, and you're looking at nearly 5,000 hours or 119 weeks of full-time work to meet one year's college costs.

I did, in fact, work when I was in college during those years. I didn't qualify for subsidized, on-campus employment because my parents had set aside too much money in my college fund by scrimping and saving. Instead, I sold shoes in nearby Harvard Square for minimum wage. One day, my roommate informed me that she had "run the numbers" on what it was costing us to be at Harvard (both our parents were so-called *full-pays*, meaning we didn't qualify for any financial aid) every hour, and she calculated that I was effectively losing money every hour I was working. Although she was probably right, I kept my fruitless job anyway, because I enjoyed it.

But stay with me. Today, it costs approximately $50,000 annually to attend a prestigious, private university like Harvard (tuition, room and board) and the minimum wage is $7.25. At that rate, it would now take a student an impossible 6,896 hours to earn that much money, the equivalent of more than three years of work (with no vacations) to pay for one year's costs. Obviously, no student can accomplish this impossible feat, and jobs are in short supply, so how do schools expect families to make up the difference? The answer is that most expect students to mortgage their futures or their parents' homes and assume ever-increasing debt loads.

FINANCIAL AID TO THE RESCUE

Once you've examined getting as many discounts to the cost of tuition as possible and the limits of supplementing your income by working a job while in school, it's time to look at one of the major sources of financial benefit—and frustration: financial aid.

REALITY RULE #11

OLD RULE:	NEW RULE:
Financial aid levels the economic playing field.	*Financial aid makes college more unaffordable. Learn the system.*

The American college financial aid system is about as mystifying as anything ever devised. Nothing else works this way.

In the normal, everyday world, you are probably used to asking the actual price of something before making a major purchase, or even a minor one, for that matter. Forget about common sense like that; it won't help you now. Your prudent everyday consumer habits are no good to you once you enter the looking-glass world of college tuition. Your only defense is learning as much as you can about the inner workings of the system, so that you can take advantage of any legal loopholes that exist to improve your chances of receiving aid and reducing your direct costs.

A story recently appeared in The University of Colorado's online newspaper entitled: "U.S. Financial Aid System Sucks and Is Stupid." Yup, that about says it all. Written by a student, this story highlights one of the biggest reasons why this horrible system has lasted for so long: Most people don't figure out how ridiculous it is until they are already in college and it is too late. The old rule or conventional belief about financial aid is that it would level the economic playing field and make college more affordable for more families. In reality, what has happened is that the financial aid system has driven tuition costs higher and made college *unaffordable* for many more people. The only way to win in this convoluted system is to learn the rules early enough to get them to work in your favor.

How Much Is Tuition . . . Really?

If you've ever taken a college tour, you may have heard a parent raise his hand and ask the guide how much the tuition is. Normally, the guide will provide the answer but then attempt to downplay the size of the figure by saying something like this: "But don't look at the sticker price . . . 50 percent (or 60, 70) of our families receive financial aid and don't pay the full cost." At this point, if you're like me, you're wondering why, if the majority of families are receiving a discount anyway, doesn't the college just lower the price.

If only it were that easy. Before any college can tell you how much tuition (and room and board, which are extra) will cost *you*, you are going to have to tell *them* how much you earn and a whole lot more. That is because the price you are going to be asked to pay depends—mainly on how much you earn, but also on how much you and your child have saved and a host of other factors. Generally speaking, the more you earn and have saved for college, the more it will cost you.

Before you can find out what *your* college bill will be, you will have to fill out what is probably the most detailed and privacy-invading financial disclosure form you will ever confront in your life: the Free Application for Federal Student Aid (FAFSA). If you are applying to an elite private institution, you will probably have to fill out a second, even more inquisitive form called the PROFILE. One parent described to me her experience filling out the PROFILE form: "They want to know everything short of how much change there is on top of your dresser right now." Some parents find the forms so overwhelming and nosy that they refuse to fill them out and give up all chance of receiving any aid. It's hard to blame them, since you have to wonder who has access to all this personal information.

It's Like Tax Planning—But Harder

Applying for financial aid is, in many ways, harder than filing your annual income taxes, because the college financial aid officers don't just want to know how much you earned last year. They also want to know how much you're worth—both parents and student. They want to know everything.

The parallels to tax planning don't end there. Everyone knows that the tax code is so complex that many families hire an accountant to give them advice and help them through it. Nevertheless, because you have to file taxes every year, and because your accountant has to explain the final figures, answer questions, and offer advice to you, over time you begin to learn something about the ins and outs of the American tax system. It becomes familiar to you. You understand that if you sold an investment home this year, it is likely to cost you money on April 15. You begin to recognize when you need to call your accountant to ask if you are making a good financial decision. Big changes to the code are debated in the media and reported widely, with plenty of notice to the public.

IF THE GROCERY STORE WORKED LIKE FINANCIAL AID

Imagine for a moment that the grocery store operated this way. You go in to buy a gallon of milk, but no one can tell you how much it will cost until you divulge your income, net worth, and accumulated assets. For those with means or who have scrimped and saved, the gallon of milk costs a lot more. It's a pretty scary thought, isn't it?

Financial aid is not like that at all. The FAFSA formula operates like a big black box. Input all (and I mean all) of your personal financial information, and out comes a magical number informing you how much the government, in its wisdom, has determined you can afford to pay next year for college. Very few people seem to wonder how the government arrives at that number, but most people are horrified when they see how much they are expected to pay.

If you had a very good year financially the year before your student starts college, then college is going to cost you more. If you have set aside a lot of money to pay for college, the price goes up instead of down.

Failure to Qualify

Above a certain income level, you are not going to qualify for any aid. You will be asked to pay the full tuition. So all the nice assurances about not looking at the sticker price won't apply to your family. As I write, that income level is probably somewhere between $180,000 and $250,000, but it also depends on a number of other factors, such as your accumulated assets.

The closest system to higher education's economic model is health care, which everyone agrees is in crisis. Health care, like college, relies upon third-party payers, called insurers, to pay part of the bill. The result is that most people have absolutely no idea how much medical procedures really cost and don't even bother to ask. When you go to get an MRI, you don't shop around for the best deal. You go wherever you want and let your insurance company handle it. The result is that the one health-care cost we all seem to agree is out of control is the expense of the insurance. So, the third-party payer drives prices upward and out of reach of more people.

This is also happening with colleges. The more financial aid that the government and the states offer, the more colleges can raise their tuition prices, because they know that the average family will not have to pay the full cost. Financial aid is supposed to make college more affordable. In fact, what it does is make college more affordable for some students while making it less affordable for others, by driving costs upward. It simply creates a different class of have-nots.

It is a pretty bad system, but at least with health care, insurance helps with the most catastrophic costs. We are all uninsured against out-of-control tuition costs. Imagine now that health care operated like the college financial aid system and your doctor just told you that you are going to require a lifesaving operation. "Oh, no!" you say. "How much is this going to cost me?" You are pleased that, with considerable foresight, you have diligently set aside a lot of money over the years preparing for just such an emergency.

The hospital administrators respond, "We have no idea what it's going to cost you, yet. First we'll need to see your tax returns, statements on all your bank accounts, documentation of all your business investments, stock values, and any other accumulated assets you may possess. We'll also need to get an appraisal on your house. The price is different for everyone and how much it is depends on how much you can afford to pay."

At this point, you might decide that it would be better to keel over with a heart attack.

With college costs, the more we save, the more the system can charge us; for the middle classes, it can be like running on a treadmill that keeps speeding up. For those in the middle, the more you hustle to meet the high price, the higher the price goes. Those who earn low incomes will qualify for substantial grants, and those who are rich can afford to buy whatever they like. Families earning between $100,000 and $200,000, however, are hit hardest of all, with little relief in sight. These are the people who, ironically, sometimes earn *too much* to afford to send their child to the college of their choice. They are considered too affluent to qualify for aid but do not make enough to pay the full price without taking a huge hit to their standard of living.

Students from these families are increasingly showing up on public college campuses, while students from families earning less can comfortably select expensive private colleges for no additional cost.

TAKE ACTION NOW TO LOWER YOUR COLLEGE COSTS

I hope I've inspired you to be proactive about curtailing your costs, because spring of a high school student's junior year is when the financial aid game begins. Your income, assets, and a student's assets all come into play at that point. It's all on the record and will be included in your final calculation. Mistakes made after this point can cost you.

The first step you must take is to figure out what your family's personal college tax is going to be. I call the financial aid calculation a *tax* because the system comes to you courtesy of the same government that created the tax code, and it essentially works the same way. Your bill, or tax, is determined annually by running your financial figures through the federal financial aid formula, which is called the Federal Methodology. Certain choices are "assessed" more highly than others. The formula has no emotions. What you get out of it depends on what you put into it.

Essentially the formula assesses the parents' income and assets, and the student's income and assets, to determine how much your family will be expected to pay for college. Depending on adjusted gross income level, the formula may determine that up to 47 percent of the parents' income is "available" to pay for college, along with 3 to 6 percent of their total assets. Mind you, the assessment on assets is for *each* school year, so if your assets are assessed at the highest rate, you will be expected to cash out nearly 25 percent of your assets by the time your child graduates. For the student, the formula may consider 50 percent of a student's income (above a small allowance) to be available for college, along with 20 percent of their assets. Again, this is annually, so a student could lose up to 80 percent of his or her assets to college (or more at a PROFILE school)—a much higher rate than the parents. The formula uses a graduated scale to assess the parents' contribution, while the student's assessment is a flat rate.

Of course, you are only going to input correct and legal information. There is no lying or omissions on federal forms. But there are legal choices available to you, and it is up to you to learn what they are and to take full advantage of them. The federal tax year that begins in January of your student's junior year of high school and ends senior year in December will determine the size of your freshman year tuition payments. The federal form comes online January 1, right after the prior tax year ends on December 31.

FILLING OUT THE FAFSA

The government's financial aid form, as I've said above, is called the Free Application for Federal Student Aid and is commonly referred to as the *FAFSA*. You can find it here: *www.fafsa.ed.gov*. It's like a tax return but even worse. Why? Because they don't just want to know how much you earned last year. They also want to know how much all of you—the parents and the student—have saved over your entire lives. Generally speaking, the more money you have set aside for college, the more you will be asked to pay, making you rightly wonder why you bothered saving. But income is going to be the biggest driver of your cost. It would be much fairer if the formula would average your income over a few years, but it doesn't. All it takes into account is the *previous year's income*. If you received a big bonus the year before college, watch out. This will swell your income and increase college costs.

The time leading up to college is really not a good time to have a great financial year. It is also a terrible time for a financial windfall, such as selling a business or a house, because sudden moves like that will make you appear richer on paper than you actually are. So be careful if any of these things are in your immediate future. If possible, take care of them before the junior year of high school or put them off.

Most families innocently sit and wait until January of their child's senior year to find out what their college tax bill will be. This is too late, because at that point there is almost nothing you can do to adjust it. The tax information from the previous year is what determines the size of the bill, so the previous year is when you need to act.

For this reason, *you need to do your own estimated FAFSA calculation early on.* I can't stress this point strongly enough. Ideally, you will do this a full year before facing the real one. You need to gain an approximation of the college costs your family will be facing and determine if there are steps you can take, while there is still time, to influence the situation in your favor. Failing to do this is like filling out your income tax form but not taking the deductions you are entitled to. It will cost you—potentially big time.

There are two ways you are going to try to approach your college costs:

1. **Maximize the amount of aid you receive. Not every family can qualify for financial aid, but more families can qualify than currently do. With adjustments to your income and asset allocation, you may be surprised to find out that you can qualify for some aid, despite a relatively high income.**

2. **Minimize your costs. *Everyone* can do this, regardless of your income and assets.**

Let's run through the steps you are going to follow.

STRATEGIES TO MAXIMIZE COLLEGE AID

STEP ONE: Run Your EFC Calculation as Early as Possible.

In financial aid-speak, *EFC* means your *Expected Family Contribution*. After you answer all of the questions on the FAFSA form, the final result will tell you how much your family is expected to pay for college next year. To be clear, the EFC is actually the *minimum* amount your family will be expected to pay. If you select a college that does not offer much financial aid, your actual costs could wind up being a good deal higher. Just because you qualify for aid doesn't mean that every college is obligated to give it to you. Poorly funded colleges are unable to offer much aid.

This EFC number determines everything and gives you your best estimate of what your actual costs will be moving forward. Do not look at college tuition prices yet; they won't help you to determine your costs because you are dealing with a third-party payer system. The EFC gives you an idea of whether or not the third party (the government) will be chipping in to help you pay and, if so, how much. Until you know what your Expected Family Contribution is, you have no idea if those tuition prices will even apply to you.

Incidentally, it is worth pointing out that *EFC* stands for Expected *Family* Contribution—not Expected *Parent* Contribution. Many students misunderstand this. The financial aid formula looks closely at the student's assets and will expect a monetary contribution toward college from her, as well. Make sure that everyone knows they are supposed to be chipping in; don't let students assume that this figure does not apply to them. In fact, assets in a child's name are counted more heavily than nearly anything else in the formula, which means that putting money in your child's name can be a big financial aid mistake.

To calculate the EFC, you are going to have to gather together pretty much all of your family's financial documents, including the student's. I know this isn't enjoyable, but trust me, it can pay off later. Even if turns out that you do not qualify for aid, you will have removed any false illusions and learned the true college costs that you are facing. This will empower you to make better decisions, moving forward.

GO ONLINE FOR HELP

Up until recently, it was very difficult to run your own EFC calculation, but there are now free online calculators that can provide you with good estimates.

I suggest you use the EFC calculator at *www.finaid.org/calculators/finaidestimate.phtml*. It allows you to run calculations using both the Federal Methodology and the Institutional Methodology, which is what the private PROFILE form uses. There is also a FAFSA Forecaster available at the FAFSA website, *www.fafsa.ed.gov* (they spell it FAFSA4caster). Also, according to the most recent Higher Education Opportunity Act, colleges themselves are now supposed to supply parents with their own online "Net Price Calculators" to provide greater transparency regarding the actual costs they are going to be expected to pay. See *www.courierpostonline.com/apps/pbcs.dll/article?AID=2011310090013*. This is a brand new, very positive development in providing greater pricing transparency to families. I suspect that the quality of these calculators will vary tremendously, though, so I still think the non-school-specific ones I recommended will be the best bet for the average family for a long while.

College is actually a great time to review all your family's financial positions and to begin planning for your next child heading to college—or for the next phase of your life. Retirement planning follows fast on the heels of college planning, and you should take it into account when deciding how much your family can afford to spend on an undergraduate degree.

What to Do with the EFC

After you run your EFC calculation, you will receive a number that you will be expected to pay next year. If your EFC is zero, which only happens for very low-income families, then your family would be expected to pay nothing for college and could expect to receive plentiful aid. Here are some sample EFCs that I ran using an online calculator:

- **Income $50,000 = EFC $5,000**

- **Income $75,000 = EFC $14,000**

- **Income $100,000 = EFC $23,000**

- **Income $150,000 = EFC $40,000**

- **Income $175,000 = EFC $48,000**

- **Income $200,000 = EFC $56,000**

- **Income $250,000 = EFC $71,000**

I did not include any assets to come up with these numbers; I only input the salary level. These are just ballpark figures to give you some idea of the numbers you might expect to see. With assets included, these numbers will rise. I stopped at $250,000 because an EFC of $71,000 would prevent a family from qualifying for need-based financial aid at every college, since there is no school in the country that costs that much annually . . . yet. Of course, there are other factors that play into the financial aid formula, but income is generally the biggest determiner of your cost.

Let's say your EFC turns out to be $20,000. This means your family will be expected to come up with that much money for the next year of college. If you do not have $20,000 on hand (and many don't) then you will be expected to borrow to come up with it. Anything above that amount will probably be awarded to you in the form of financial aid grants and loans that the student will be expected to repay. The proportions of awarded gift aid (grants) versus self-help (work-study and loans) will vary considerably from school to school. Therefore, if a family with an EFC of $20,000 is sending a child to a college that costs $50,000 annually, they would need $30,000 in financial aid—that is, assuming the college meets 100 percent of financial need. Not all schools meet all your financial need as demonstrated by the FAFSA form, but the well-endowed schools do so. You can find a list of college endowments at *www.en.wikipedia.org/wiki/list _of_colleges_and_universities_in_the_united_states_by_ endowment*. Harvard has the biggest endowment and offers the most generous aid. All the Ivies are well-endowed. A few big name schools have surprisingly low endowments, such as Georgetown and George Washington University. They will likely be less generous with aid and leave students with a lot of debt.

The true cost of a college is called the *cost of attendance*, which is sometimes abbreviated COA. The cost of attendance includes everything from tuition and room and board to books, supplies, personal expenses, and even some travel back and forth to school. It is nice that colleges tend to be all-inclusive in setting this figure, because it helps to eliminate expensive surprises later on.

Now, what if you run your calculation and find that your EFC is $50,000, but you are looking at a school that costs $44,000? In that case, you would be considered to have no need and be what is known in college financial lingo as a *full-pay*. The sticker price of the school would be the actual price for you.

It is possible for the same family to qualify for aid at one school and to be considered no-need, full-pay at another. It depends on the tuition price. This is why a family with a low EFC can often afford to send a child anywhere, but a middle-class family with a mid-range EFC is much more cost-sensitive. This is also why some high-priced private colleges are seeing a donut-hole appear in their enrollments, with high- and low-income students attending but very few in the middle. This is a growing problem at many pricey colleges. It can lead to an unsettling Rich/Poor divide in the student population at those institutions that is certainly not fully representative of true economic diversity in the country. What is increasingly missing is the struggling middle class.

STEP TWO: Don't Panic. Run It Again, Using New Data.

If you are like most people, when you see your EFC it is so high that you feel a little lightheaded and may need to sit down. Don't panic, yet. It is possible that you can lower it by making some changes. Let's do a little creative thinking here and try to figure out why your number is so high.

Income

Is it your income? If you are earning over $250,000 a year, then you probably suspected that you would not be receiving much financial aid for college. But if you earn less than that, it could be your assets that are driving your cost up so high. What are some of these assets?

Money in Your Child's Name

Money held in a child's name is one of the biggest factors that can cause a super-high EFC. The financial aid formula assumes that money in a child's name is meant to be spent on college, so it "taxes" or "assesses" it at a much higher rate than money that is held in a parent's name. If your accountant advised you to save money in a child's name for tax purposes, he probably did not understand the potential financial aid implications of this recommendation. Luckily, if you have run your college financial aid estimate early enough, there is time to shift assets so as to reduce your EFC.

Cash on Hand

Do you have a substantial amount of money sitting in savings or checking accounts? If you leave it sitting in those accounts, then the formula raises the amount you will be expected to pay. Basically, if the formula sees money, it adds it in. This is how the formula thinks: See money, take money.

You want to lose the liquid cash. Precollege is a great time to take that money and pay down your household debt. This is much better, from a financial aid perspective, than leaving cash sitting in savings. Incidentally, the financial formula does not ask about your debt. It only cares about what you have now, not about what you owe. For that reason, you might also want to consider paying down your mortgage. (An important caveat: The FAFSA does not consider home equity in assessing your assets. Schools that distribute their own institutional endowment funds, however, also use the PROFILE form to calculate your aid-eligibility. This formula *does* count home equity. To see a list of schools requiring this second form, go to *www.collegeboard.org/* and search "PROFILE participating institutions.")

In the financial aid formula, some assets are assessed and others are not. For example, your retirement accounts are not assessed, while your savings accounts are. Obviously, shifting funds from savings to retirement will improve your financial aid eligibility. Personal property is also not assessed. This means that if a student needs a car to attend college, you will want to take the cash out of savings and make that purchase before filling out the FAFSA form. The same goes for a computer. You should spend the money on these necessary items *before* filling out the form, not after.

Now you are going to run and re-run that EFC calculation using every different possible financial scenario you can come up with. What if Mom went back to work? What if Dad or Mom stopped working? What if we sold our stocks and paid off the house? What if we moved cash into retirement accounts?

Get creative and use blue-sky thinking. Try every possibility you can come up with. Try everything you can think of to lower the EFC to the point where you can qualify for some financial aid.

Most families try to think of ways to earn more money during college years. It makes sense: If we earn more money, we will have more money for college. But now I'm telling you to act against reason and stop thinking that way! You've gone through the looking glass, remember? Earning extra money at this point will help only if you are sure you are not going to qualify for any aid whatsoever. If you do qualify for some aid, then you might actually qualify for even *more* if one parent takes a hiatus from work during college. Yes, that's right. Less money equals more money. Try plugging those numbers into the FAFSA calculation to see what your family contribution would be on a single income. You might be surprised.

Income is the main driver of what you will be required to pay, so think counterintuitively: less income good, more income bad. If you're a parent of a college-bound student, this could turn out to be a great time to consider starting a business, shifting careers, or even going back to school yourself. The only way to find out what effect those alternatives will have on your chances of receiving aid is to run the numbers.

Two at Once?

Can you possibly arrange things so that you can have two children in college at the same time? It makes some sense, if two students are close in age, to have the older one wait a year or so until they're both ready to enter college. This is because one of the little-known quirks of the financial aid system is that the parents' expected contribution for the upcoming year stays roughly the same no matter how many kids you have in college. A family with one child who has an EFC of $70,000 is not going to get financial aid, anywhere. But if the mother of sextuplets had an EFC of $70,000, she could conceivably send her children to school for the same amount as sending one! In other words, if children in the same family are four years apart, and your EFC is $50,000, then you can expect to pay that amount for eight years straight, until both of them are through college. But . . . if they were twins, you could wind up paying $50,000 for only four years—an incredible 50 percent discount. The EFC barely changes.

Take a close look at each of the questions on the FAFSA form or in the EFC calculator and play around with each of those factors. See how much difference they make for your family. Generally speaking, you want to appear as poor as you possibly can on paper, but you can't falsify information. You can, however, juggle your asset allocations.

BE AWARE OF TIMING

Did you sell a house or a business or have a large cash windfall, such as an inheritance? This shows up as available income. For financial aid purposes, it's best to hunker down and avoid making any sudden moves during the four years a student is in college. However, "the four years a student is in college" begin earlier than you probably expect. Spring of a student's junior year of high school is when the aid formula begins taking account of your financial circumstances to determine freshman college costs. You will want to continue to be mindful of the financial aid implications of any monetary decisions through December of the junior year of college, because your aid eligibility must be recalculated each year, using new tax returns. After spring (January) of the junior year of college, you can do anything financially you want to do, because your personal finances are no longer under college scrutiny. (That is, unless you have a younger child getting ready for college.) Basically, the financial aid process starts and ends a year earlier than most people realize.

In some cases, families have lowered their EFC by tens of thousands of dollars with a simple change in how assets are held. Sometimes, if you do something as simple as switching the residence of a child in a divorce situation to an unemployed parent's address, you can change your family from full-pay to "zero expected contribution." Again, you can't misrepresent the facts on the form: If you say that a student lived with one parent for most of the year, then that has to be the truth. You will need to sign this form and attest that all the information you supply is correct.

STEP THREE: Shift Assets.

At this point, if you have determined that making adjustments to your financial situation may increase your chances of receiving aid, it is time to talk to your financial adviser to see if there would be any penalties or tax consequences for making changes to your overall financial picture. For example, some parents employ what are called 529 accounts (or plans). These are education savings devices operated by the state or by educational institutions and are designed to help parents set aside money against the future cost of sending their child to college. Although the plan has tax benefits, moving money out of 529 accounts may carry a penalty. This is one of the reasons I don't like them. A second reason I dislike them is because they are assessed in the financial aid formula. (For more information on 529 plans, go to *www.savingforcollege.com*.)

If you have a trust fund for a student and determine that it makes sense to change the way these assets are held, you must follow legal requirements. Likewise, you could incur tax consequences for selling other investments. So, explore all of the ramifications and weigh them against potential gains in aid eligibility. It may turn out that the possible benefits of making changes will be outweighed by the penalties associated with closing certain accounts, but there is only one way to find out. You have to get the answers and run the numbers. In doing this, you will probably want to speak to an accountant, financial planner, or trusted adviser. There are also college planners who specialize in financial plans for college, such as Planet Tuition, which includes former college financial aid officers (see *www .planettuition.com*).

I can't give you overly specific advice here, because every family's situation is unique. But just to give you an idea of how much it can pay off, I have seen situations in which a family was able to reduce an EFC by $20,000 per year or more by making very simple, legal changes to investments. That's over $80,000 in potential savings per kid, just by doing a little homework and a bit of legwork.

STRATEGIES TO MINIMIZE COLLEGE COSTS

Once you run an EFC estimate, you should have a pretty good idea whether you are going to be considered an aid-eligible family or a so-called *full-pay*. Now you are going to shift to the second stage of your college savings plan: reducing college costs. At this point, your strategies will diverge, depending on whether or not you can expect to receive financial aid.

Aid-Eligible Family

Begin the process of reducing college costs by seeking colleges that award the most generous aid. It won't help you much to be in a position to receive financial aid if you select a school that doesn't offer much. Colleges offer a wide range of assistance in meeting demonstrated financial need, although the most well-known schools tend to have the best reputations in this area. Generally speaking, schools that are well endowed can afford to offer the most generous financial aid. Just to give you a sense, here are the ten schools with the highest endowments in the United States, all in the billions.

1. **Harvard**

2. **Yale**

3. **Princeton**

4. **University of Texas**

5. **MIT**

6. **University of Michigan**

7. **Columbia**

8. **University of Pennsylvania**

9. **Northwestern**

10. **Texas A&M**

To get an idea of your financial aid prospects at other schools, use *www.collegeboard.org*. Enter the name of the school you are considering, and then click on "Financial Aid." You are looking for schools that meet 100 percent of need.

Even though you have created a list of schools that meet all of your need, you are not finished. That is because schools can claim they are meeting all of your financial need when, in fact, they are awarding mainly loans. So, you also want to look at any information provided that indicates what percentage of that offered aid comes in the form of grants (which you don't have to pay back) and what percentage is self-help. *Self-help* means loans and work-study.

Obviously, grants are the more desirable form of financial aid. If you can't find this information online (some schools do not want to publish it), call the school's financial aid office and ask them directly.

You might think that you can reduce the amount of loans your student will have to take out by chasing scholarships sponsored by the local Rotary Club or other civic organizations to supplement your aid award. Think again. Generally speaking, this will probably turn out to be a waste of your time and energy, since an aid family that receives outside money for college will most likely simply lose a corresponding amount of federal or school aid. Sadly, this is a disincentive for an aid-eligible family to make the effort to apply for scholarships.

Don't think you can keep an outside scholarship secret from the college, either. When you accept your financial aid award, you agree that you will inform the financial aid office of any other money that comes into your possession. You could get into big trouble for withholding that information. For this reason financial aid officers conduct searches on published newspaper articles to find stories about scholarship awards.

You still want to minimize your loans as much as possible. You might do this by expecting the student to work to earn more money, but here again, above a pretty low salary threshold, this won't help much. Once a student passes $3,000 in income, the formula adds fifty cents of every dollar to the amount he is expected to pay next year. In essence, you lose aid. A student is really helping the school by working to earn money beyond that threshold, rather than improving his own financial situation. After he reaches the cut-off, he is probably better off spending extra time studying to get better grades or taking additional courses to finish school more quickly.

Full-Pay Family

If it is clear you are not going to receive financial aid because your expected family contribution is high, then you must look very closely at each school's sticker price and ask yourself how much you can realistically afford to pay for college. Once you are sure you are in the full-pay category, it obviously helps to have as much liquid savings and income as possible to attempt to meet costs. The rules are completely different for those who will receive no aid, which is why it is so important to run the actual numbers through the formula to determine which strategies apply to your family. The earlier you do this the better, so that you know your game plan moving forward.

The unfair reality is that full-pay families may have to look at schools that cost less than those that students receiving aid can comfortably select. Some schools may be out of your reach, financially, unless money truly is no object for you. You will have to make that determination for yourself, although I will offer you some guidelines to consider.

Search for Scholarships

To minimize costs, a full-pay family may need to seek schools with affordable tuition. This means considering public universities and community colleges. Because you are in the position of paying the full cost of college with no financial aid, any outside scholarships you receive will directly reduce your tuition cost. So, students of full-pay families will want to seek as much scholarship money as possible.

Unfortunately, the emergence of need-based financial aid has placed a serious dent in the world of scholarships. Many awarding agencies seem to have figured out that the money they award often merely serves to reduce aid packages (and assist the college) rather than going directly to the student. However, this is not true for full-pay families. Every dollar a full-pay family receives in scholarships will directly reduce their cost of attendance.

Many families harbor the illusion that there are plentiful scholarship dollars out there somewhere. I wish it were so. A great deal of confusion about scholarships stems from the fact that colleges sometimes refer to need-based aid as *scholarships*. The reality is that the overwhelming majority of college aid today is based on need rather than academic, athletic, or musical achievement. However, full-pay students should still make the effort to seek out existing private scholarship opportunities. The best place to start is with your high school guidance office and by contacting any awarding organizations with which family members are affiliated.

Transfer Options

A student determined to graduate from a private, expensive, name-brand school should at least consider two-year transfer options from less expensive public or community colleges. This could conceivably shave nearly $100,000 from the total tuition bill, while the final degree will be exactly the same. This is a very smart strategy; more students should take advantage of cost-effective transfer opportunities. I am currently seeing an alarming trend: students transferring *out* of their expensive dream colleges after a year or two as they become overwhelmed by the accumulating cost, and switching to less expensive publics. Those students make the expensive mistake of paying a high cost for the early credits at the name-brand school, but receiving their diploma from a less prestigious one. This is the reverse of what families should be doing.

Of course, every student transferring out of a private institution makes room for one to transfer in. So, economic downturns such as the one in 2008–2009 create some tremendous transfer opportunities for cost-conscious students.

Finally, both aid-eligible and full-pay families need to limit the amount of loans they assume, for obvious reasons. As much as possible, pay as you go and try to stick to low-interest, subsidized loans. Relying mainly on unsubsidized loans is a warning sign that you may be getting in over your head, financially. Financing college with debt just compounds the overall affordability problem.

WHEN TO SAY: "WE CAN'T AFFORD IT"

Sometimes, even when you qualify for some financial aid, the deal is just not good enough. You've tried everything you can to lower your costs and still don't see how you are going to make things work financially. No one wants to face their financial limitations and give up the first choice dream school, but sometimes, this is the best option for everyone's long-term financial security and peace of mind. Here are my suggestions for when you should pull the plug and choose a less expensive school:

1. **If you are thinking of re-mortgaging your home to pay for tuition**

2. **If you are thinking of cashing in your retirement accounts or stopping your annual contributions to pay for tuition**

3. **If you are pretty sure there is no way you will be able to afford all four years at the college and your child will have to transfer out eventually**

4. **If you are going to be losing sleep or risking your emotional health over the size of the tuition or loan payments**

5. **If you have to borrow to pay for freshman year or to reach your EFC**

6. **If you have to rely on high interest, unsubsidized loans to pay for tuition.**

These are all signs that you are in over your head. It is okay to walk away from a bad financial deal.

It is also okay for a high school student to hear the words: "We can't afford it." She will recover from that news far faster than she will recover from decades of unaffordable loan payments. Rest assured that a student can still achieve all of her goals and career aspirations at an affordable school. Remember, also, that every dollar parents spend on college cannot be spent later to help a child buy a home, pay for graduate school, or pursue other goals that will arise after college. Saying "yes" now will increase the likelihood parents will have to say "no," later. You have to think long-term about how your family's limited assets can be best deployed to finance *all* the dreams that lie in the future . . . not just for the next four years. Here is a chart depicting your college financial strategies, in condensed form:

STRATEGIES TO MAXIMIZE COLLEGE AID

STEP 1: Run your EFC calculation as early as possible

STEP 2: Run it again, using different numbers

STEP 3: Shift assets if it will lower your EFC below cost of attendance

AID-ELIGIBLE

If your EFC is less than the college cost, you can expect to receive some discounts.

FULL-PAY

If your EFC is more than the college cost, you will have to pay the full amount.

STRATEGIES TO MINIMIZE COLLEGE COST

AID-ELIGIBLE

- Seek schools that offer the most aid
- Find schools with the best ratio of grants to loans
- Scholarships can reduce your aid
- Minimize loans

FULL-PAY

- Seek schools with affordable tuition
- Look into transfer options
- Seek scholarships
- Minimize loans

EVERY FAMILY

- Seek merit aid
- Reduce time to graduation
- Max out on AP, IB, and dual enrollment credits in high school
- Max out on CLEP credits in college

SHAVE THOUSANDS OFF YOUR COLLEGE BILL

Once you've gone through the various steps outlined above, are you done? No, not quite. There are some other strategies and tactics you can employ to keep chipping away at that stubborn invoice for college.

Merit Aid: The Brightest Light in College Funding

As I have explained, most college financial aid is awarded based on need, which is determined by the FAFSA form. Colleges typically expect families who do not qualify for financial aid to pay the full cost of attendance. The one exception, and the brightest light in the modern world of college funding, is merit aid.

Colleges award merit aid to incoming students based on their accomplishments. Merit can be academic, athletic, or based on some other talent or attribute that the student brings to the college. *Merit aid does not need to be repaid*; it is one way that schools discount their prices to encourage strong candidates to enroll.

Every college applicant should seek as much merit aid as possible. A good rule of thumb to follow is that you are more likely to qualify if you are in the top 10 percent of students at that school. Often, students want to attend the most selective school they can squeak into, but their chances of receiving merit aid will be best at colleges where they will be at the top of their class. Generally speaking, merit aid opportunities are most plentiful at nonelite private colleges. Some public colleges and universities have impressive merit aid programs, as well—often aligned with their Honors Colleges. Unfortunately, the Ivies and a few other highly selective schools do not offer any merit aid. Instead, they are extremely generous with need-based aid.

Applying for Merit Aid

Currently, there is no centralized way to apply for merit aid or even to figure out how much is out there. One website attempting to consolidate some of this information is *www.meritaid .com*. For now, the best strategy for locating merit aid is to narrow down your list of schools and then visit each school's website and search individually for "Merit Aid," "Merit Scholarships," or just "Scholarships."

The guidelines for receiving a merit-based award vary considerably, depending on the selectivity of the school. Many colleges will tell you that their merit aid is awarded through an ambiguous competitive process with no set guidelines. In essence, they are saying that it depends on the quality of each year's applicant pool and they don't want to commit to a specific amount of money for students who meet certain criteria.

Other schools, however, are explicit in announcing exactly what grades and test scores will qualify an applicant for a precise amount of merit award. Some even have handy calculators posted on their websites telling families exactly how much merit aid a student with a certain GPA and test scores can expect. You simply enter the student's academic information, and the calculator tells you how much money that student will receive. Schools do this to encourage good students to apply and to motivate students, once there, to study and do well. Merit aid awards are definitely worth pursuing, particularly if your student is a high achiever likely to appeal to numerous colleges. At most colleges, the admissions or athletic offices award merit aid while the financial aid office handles need-based aid.

THE TRUTH ABOUT
FINANCIAL AID OFFICERS

REALITY RULE #12

OLD RULE:	NEW RULE:
Rely on the financial aid office to help you figure out how to pay for college.	*Financial aid officers work for the college. Do your own research.*

Asking a financial aid officer if you can afford to attend the college she works for is a lot like asking a mortgage broker if you can afford a particular house or asking a car salesman if you can afford to buy a nice, new car. The answer will always be "yes"; they will happily work out the payment schedule and figure out the number of years you will be indebted to them. Their job is to help you finance the purchase—not to ensure you get a good deal.

It is imperative that you make your decisions about how much college you can afford independently of the financial aid office's recommendations. Financial aid officers are looking out for their own institution's bottom line. It's up to you to look after yours.

One of the main duties of financial aid officers is to help students receive all the federal and state grants for which they qualify. After all, this means outside money coming in to the institution. To do this, they have to follow certain rules; beyond that, their hands are tied. They may have some limited discretion with the distribution of institutional funds, but they certainly have no vested interest in helping your family save money, because their salaries are paid by the institution, not by you. However nice they may seem, ultimately, remember: *They are not working for you; they are working for the school.* For this reason, financial aid officers tend to be guarded about sharing information that might potentially increase aid awards.

You Have a Right to Know

I had a revelatory moment concerning financial aid when I worked in college admissions. This incident bothers me to this day and certainly influenced my opinion on the subject. A divorced father came to me privately and said that his daughter had been accepted to our school with a generous financial aid package. He said that he had been saving money over the years in preparation for this moment and wanted to help pay her tuition, but he was concerned that his contributions would adversely affect her financial aid award. He asked me if his suspicions were correct, and I answered that I didn't know, but I would help him find out.

I went to another admissions counselor who had once worked in financial aid and posed his question to her in his presence. She hemmed and hawed for a while and refused to give him a straight answer. I was embarrassed to send him on his way without a clear response to his simple question. After he departed, this representative stormed into my office and berated me for having placed her in that situation. Her view was that he was not entitled to that information, because it might influence what he did with his money.

I responded that I thought he was entitled to know the truth and to have a direct answer to his reasonable request for factual information. He was asking what the stipulations of the financial aid formula are so that he could adhere to them and make responsible decisions moving forward. She vehemently disagreed and proceeded to insult me. To this day, I am still floored by her reaction. Her thinking is so antithetical to my own that I cannot even begin to understand it.

BE NICE TO YOUR
FINANCIAL AID OFFICER

Most financial aid officers are nice people who are simply doing their jobs. As overwhelming—and frightening—as this whole college financing process is, please resist the urge to take your frustrations out on them. I once spoke to a financial aid officer who told me that he could not begin to count the number of times he had picked up the phone and heard a curse as the first word out of the mouth of the person on the other end of the line. Obviously, these profane callers are parents who have just opened up their financial aid awards and are not pleased. Despite disappointments, cursing at college employees is abusive, not to mention counterproductive, since they hold the purse strings. Financial aid officers do have some limited discretion in their aid awards, and screaming at them certainly will not endear you to them or increase a student's chances of receiving more generous aid.

To me, her position is no different from insisting that tax-payers have no right to know what the American tax code is. Of course, withholding this information sounds absurd on its face. The American tax code is public information, and changes to it are loudly and publicly debated and widely announced. This knowledge empowers taxpayers to make financial decisions based on what is in their own best interests, within legal boundaries.

Tuition payers have rights to information and answers to their questions, too. The recent federal legislation requiring colleges to begin posting price calculators on their websites is a victory in this battle for full disclosure. The American financial aid system is, or should be, a matter of public record. Unfortunately, many prefer to have it remain a closely guarded secret. They seem to believe that it is reasonable for government bureau-crats (or an invisible computer program) to insist that families tell everything about their personal financial situation and in return to be given only as much information as the financial office wishes to divulge. Families are expected to comply with the notion that a mysterious but benevolent agency will input their data into the magical black box while they wait passively for the results.

What They Will and Won't Say

The bottom line is this: Financial aid officers will tell you what grants and loans you qualify for, but they are not responsible for helping you to arrange your finances in such a way so as to maximize your aid eligibility. In fact, they may actually try to withhold this information from you, since from their point of view you're in competition with other families, and with themselves for a piece of the institution's financial pie.

GETTING YOUR FINANCIAL AID PACKAGE

REALITY RULE #13

OLD RULE:	NEW RULE:
Financial aid is distributed equitably.	*Be first in line for aid, because it is first come, first served.*

In a fair world, financial aid resources would all be distributed equitably and everyone who qualified for them would receive them. But this isn't a fair world. You must do everything you can to improve your family's chances of receiving as much financial aid as possible, and that includes lining up quickly for it.

Many factors influence the amount of aid that a family will receive from a college. Timing is one of them. Take a look at the calendar that dominates the college admissions and aid application processes and you will notice some interesting and contradictory things.

THE IRRATIONALITY OF THE SYSTEM

The first thing you will notice is that the admissions process comes first, chronologically. This means that a student must decide to apply to a school, fill out the required application, write the essays, send his grades and test scores, and secure the necessary letters of recommendation—all before hearing a final offer on price. When was the last time you negotiated a major purchase when price was the last thing discussed?

Imagine for a moment that purchasing a home worked this way. You'd begin your shopping adventure with absolutely no idea of what you could afford or what your payments might look like, but you'd still look at every house on the market, regardless of cost. The sales professionals would even advise you not to look at the sticker price, because you might qualify for aid to help you with the purchase. Don't worry about how expensive it is, the nice sales officer would say, because hardly anyone actually pays that and we have people whose job it is to ensure you get help with financing if you are selected to own this home. You'd then submit your offer and tell the sellers that you were very, very interested in buying. At this point, your heart would be set on that 5,000 square foot ivy-covered colonial on the corner lot in the nicest part of town! You'd even tell all your friends about it and begin making plans for your new life there. Emotionally, you'd be sold.

Then, after the offer was in and the exhilarating selection process was complete, you'd begin the financial qualification process to see if you could actually afford to buy it.

This scenario is patently ridiculous, which is why this is not how the home-buying business works. Instead, you go through an approval process to prequalify for a mortgage, so that you know how much you can spend before you begin shopping; this determines the price range of homes that the realtor will show you. The process ensures that buyers make realistic choices. It also protects sellers from wasting their time on offers from those unqualified to handle the long-term payments.

Of course, the mortgage qualification process broke down during the lead-up to the housing crisis, as families were qualified for loans they could not really afford. The resulting disaster shook the foundations of the entire world's financial system. Now the housing lenders have been forced to return to strict guidelines, and qualifying for a mortgage is more difficult again—as it should be.

The same sort of prudence and circumspection needs to be applied to the whole teetering student loan industry. Instead, when it comes to finding a college families receive the kind of advice that banks were doling out to prospective home buyers before 2008: Don't limit yourself! You may qualify for a lot of financial aid! The result is that the vast majority of families go college shopping as though money is no object, only to wind up in trouble later.

Now look again at the illogic of the financial aid calendar. In most cases by December 31 students click "Send" on their college applications. Now the waiting begins. In the meantime, these anxious students go to high school wearing overpriced sweatshirts (some go for $80!) purchased from the college bookstore of Dream College and fall asleep at night under a blanket featuring the university logo. They have made the college's website their homepage and the school mascot is the backdrop on their computer screens. Now that they have their emotional college selections, and you're all waiting to see if you get the fat envelope in the mail . . . *now* . . . you're going to begin the process of finding out if you can afford it!

Filing a Corrected FAFSA

The federal FAFSA form comes online on January 1. Many schools have financial aid priority application deadlines around March 1. Filling out the FAFSA form requires the average family to have already filled out their federal taxes, which as you know, are not due until April 15. In many cases, families are still waiting for required documentation from financial institutions in March. When you receive these documents is largely outside of your control. Nevertheless, you are expected to fill out this form and answer questions for which you lack the needed paperwork.

What is a family to do? As impossible as it sounds, the answer is to fill out the financial aid form anyway, using guesstimates, then file a second corrected FAFSA later, after your tax information is available. It's a huge inconvenience, wildly inefficient, and a tremendous waste of everyone's time, but you need to do it because you need to stake your claim to the existing financial aid dollars at a student's school. The sad truth is, even if you do qualify for aid on the FAFSA form, that alone does not guarantee that you will receive it. You are not going to get any aid if a school has already distributed all of its available funds. The rule is, first come, first served. So get in line and save your place early.

The Hazards of "Gapping" and How to Avoid Them

Financial aid awards are often used to encourage attendance. Highly desirable students may be given much more favorable packages than other students who may be "gapped." *Aid gapping* means that a college fails to meet all of a student's financial need. The school leaves a gap between the amount of aid you need and how much it actually awards you. For instance, a student may have $20,000 worth of demonstrated need according to the FAFSA, but the school is only willing to meet $10,000 of it, either because they simply don't have any more money or they are unwilling to give any more to this particular student. They leave the parents to make up the difference.

Certain colleges are known for gapping—particularly those with small endowments. Here is a list of schools leaving students with the most debt: *www.forbes.com/2010/11/04/highest-debt-college-students-american-university.html*. As well, here's a bit more on "gapping": *www.insidehighered.com/news/2008/11/26/aid*. Many schools do it because they can get away with it, as they have a long line of well-to-do students willing and able to pay the full price. The practice of aid gapping is a not-so-subtle message telling your family that you might seriously want to consider enrolling your student elsewhere. The message is, "Hey . . . we'll take your student, but only if you pay through the nose."

I've known families who began cashing in retirement accounts and mortgaging their residence to fill in the gap. I wouldn't recommend this. I believe you should "vote with your feet" and walk away from bad deals. The sooner people do this, the sooner the college bubble will begin deflating. On the other hand, schools that really want a particular student may meet more than the demonstrated need or reduce the amount of loans and increase the grants, making a student's cost of attendance affordable. These are the deals you want to find.

A WORD ON WAITING LISTS

In recent years, college waiting lists have been growing longer. There are several reasons for this; one of the main ones is that finances are driving many college decisions now, and more students are turning down schools they like but just can't afford. Waiting lists are one of the ways that colleges reduce their own uncertainty levels and fill their incoming classes. Unfortunately, one common stipulation of remaining on a waiting list is that you must go to the very end of the line for limited financial aid funds. Please bear this in mind as you make your final college decisions.

CHAPTER 7

MINIMIZING YOUR COLLEGE INVESTMENT

REALITY RULE #14

OLD RULE:	NEW RULE:
Student loans are "good debt."	*Base your college borrowing on your expected entry-level earnings.*

For years, the conventional wisdom assured families that student loans should be considered "good debt" because graduates would easily be able to repay them with the higher salaries they would command. Of all the old rules of college, this is probably the one with the potential to cause the most mischief, given the now-universally recognized hazards of borrowing excessive amounts of money. College debt is a problem that has snuck up on this generation of students and parents, since college costs and attendance patterns have grown incrementally while our attitudes and belief systems have remained steady.

There may have been some truth to the old rule at one time, when a college degree still set a graduate head and shoulders above others in the job market. In the past, when college costs were more reasonable and employment for graduates more certain, the idea that borrowing money to fund an education was always a wise decision held validity. Wasn't it Ben Franklin who once sagely advised that, "An investment in education always pays the best interest?"

Of course, old Ben didn't know anything about student loans. When he spoke of investment in education, he was surely speaking of investing those "pennies saved" that are "pennies earned." Debt was anathema to him. After all, he also warned, "Think what you do when you run in debt; you give to another power over your liberty."

As a potential borrower today you must seriously consider your ability to repay your student loans, given the exorbitant costs and diminished job prospects you are facing. You must recognize the crimp (more like an enormous dent!) too much debt will place upon your adult lifestyle.

College loans are not simply for a few thousand dollars, anymore; for students today, they often amount to tens of thousands of dollars of debt. For a few hapless graduates, undergraduate debt is now even reaching six figures! This is the size of debt you owe on a mortgage—but without a house to live in. Is it any wonder that one columnist recently referred to student debt as a modern form of indentured servitude? Student loan obligations can prevent graduates from beginning their adult lives. Before they even leave home, many college-bound students strap on a heavy yoke of debt that they will wear and service most of their adult lives. Many will still be making payments on their student loans when their own children are in college.

Debt Drives Students Home

Young, and not-so-young, graduates are moving back home, and delaying marriage and postponing children if they do manage to leave the nest. Student debt loads will interfere with their ability to obtain mortgages and start businesses when they wish to do so. Even worse, approximately 50 percent of college students do not even manage to graduate (that figure is even higher for minorities), yet those student loans must still be repaid regardless of their failure to obtain a degree. Having student loans with no degree is a worst-case scenario. Astonishingly, one in five federal student loans goes into default—a rate that rivals subprime mortgages.

Recently, flipping through my local newspaper, I stumbled upon a telling sign of the times. Once a week, this paper publishes a section written by and for teenagers; the editors pose a question to several students at different local high schools and print their responses. On this particular day, the question was: "Where do you see yourself in five years?" Nearly all of the students replied that they saw themselves in college or some other type of postsecondary education.

=== **COLLEGE BY THE NUMBERS** ===

Here's a very alarming fact. For some families, the biggest cost of a college education may be the interest on the student loans. Yes, interest on student loans that are amortized over ten, twenty, or even thirty years can eventually exceed the initial tuition charges.

$

One student's reply stood out, however. She said that she saw herself "graduating from college, in a huge amount of debt, and hopefully able to find a job." This student actually envisions a future for herself that includes starting out adult life deep in the red, as though this is now a completely accepted fact of life for teenagers and young adults. What a sad commentary on the plight of modern youth in America!

Student loans are such a profitable business that even prestigious, prominent higher education institutions have entered into inappropriate agreements where they receive financial benefits for recommending "preferred lenders." It's so lucrative, that the federal government is now taking it over and planning to use some of the proceeds they receive to help fund the proposed health-care expansion and other initiatives. According to Former U.S. Education Secretary and Senator Lamar Alexander, this is how it will work: "The federal government will borrow money at 2.8 percent and then lend it to students at 6.8 percent—spending the difference on health care and new government programs." He argues that this is unfair to younger generations and proposed an amendment to prohibit overcharging students to fund programs other than higher education. You may rightly wonder why the interest received from student loans is not going to be used to reduce the cost of college, instead.

Parents and students need only visit *www.projectonstudent debt.org* and its associated Facebook page (*www.facebook.com/pages/the-institute-for-college-access-success/15618662356*) to read countless tales of woe regarding the damage that un-payable amounts of student debt are wreaking on today's college graduates. These stories of financial struggle ought to serve as modern-day cautionary tales:

"That 26k in student loans in the 1980s has ballooned to 70k with interest . . ."

"I honestly thought that if I just went to school and got that stupid sheet of paper with my name on it all of my simplistic dreams would just magically come true, because surely the Government wouldn't set me up to fail so massively with loans that are supposed to AID you . . ."

"I paid for my associates degree with part time jobs. But I acquired $90K in private student loans completing my four-year degree at a private university. I'm lucky I have a job to cover my monthly $920 student loan payment. But I live paycheck to paycheck. I've accepted that I won't own a home anytime soon. I can't save money because most of it goes toward paying student loans and credit card debt . . ."

The stories go on and on and on. More than one graduate even admits contemplating suicide over the amount of debt and her inability to pay it. Others consider dropping off the grid or leaving the country, like fugitives. This is surely the American Dream turned into a nightmare.

Similarly, *The Huffington Post* hosts an ongoing series called "Share Your Story—Majoring in Debt." Like a modern day confessional, stunned graduates come to tell their tales, unburden their souls, and express lamentations. There is Jennifer Dessinger who is $177,250 in debt; James Moreau who is $120,000 in debt; Maureen Arthurs who is $26,000 in debt; and Scott Adams who is $55,000 in debt.

The students even share their photographs while holding cards in front of themselves displaying the shocking totals. The pictures resemble criminal mugshots, although their only crime was seeking an education. Most convey profound regret and confide that they feel they have made a big mistake with their young lives. All are suffering from borrower's remorse. Every student and parent should review this website before agreeing to take on any student loans to finance college education. Forewarned is forearmed.

AMERICA'S YOUTH IN TROUBLE

Adding to the terrible strain of debt is the inability of many students to obtain entry-level positions in their careers. Economic and demographic conditions have the current crop of college graduates trapped under a gray ceiling of aging baby boomers, many of whom are unwilling to leave the job market and some of whom are taking low-level jobs typically reserved for entry-level workers. The Great Recession appears to be hitting young people the hardest, and they have no financial reserves to fall back on, aside from their already cash-strapped parents.

According to a *New York Times* article, "American Dream Elusive for Millennials," the prospects for young adults in the workplace have "rarely been so bleak." The *Times* reports that their unemployment rates are "reminiscent of the 1930s."

The New York Post, in "The Dead End Kids: Young, Unemployed, and Facing a Tough Future" claims that, "The number of young Americans without a job has exploded to 53.4 percent—a post–World War II high, according to the Labor Department." Today, the chances of a young graduate finding a job with a living wage are slim, indeed. Must today's young adults really deal with crushing debt loads on top of the other stiff odds in life they currently face?

Loans Can Be a Trap

College students are probably the most vulnerable borrowers in the country, since they are still in their teenage years and by definition not yet educated. Debt for someone so young and inexperienced should be pursued with the utmost caution and undertaken in the smallest amounts possible. College applicants are extremely susceptible to the persuasion of their elders, and they can easily buy into the hype and mythology surrounding college. In high school, in the movies, and in thousands of brochures that begin hitting their mailboxes during junior year they see how college attendance is celebrated and idealized. Everyone else is doing it. Why not them? How could they possibly lose?

Student loans are very easy to obtain. If a student has a pulse, he can get a student loan, regardless of the fact that he has no credit history. In fact, most schools practically throw them at you and even come chasing after you to take them. My daughter's college contacted us repeatedly, by mail and e-mail, to come and get her student loans, even though we had never asked for any. (We were required to complete the FAFSA as a precondition of receiving her merit award. In the process, we apparently qualified for some unsubsidized loans.) We threw all these loan letters in the garbage without opening them. After she enrolled, in mid-October, I received an urgent e-mail from the college saying they hadn't received her "loan money" yet. I called the billing office, and they informed me that they were expecting to receive money from our student loans. I informed them that I had never requested a loan, and had no intention of taking one. "Oh," she replied. "Then you'll have to go to our website and reject the loan."

Astonishingly, the school had awarded the loan with no agreement from us, and it was up to me to formally reject it! In other words, the foregone conclusion was that we would receive this loan, until I explicitly told them "no." No wonder students wind up in so much financial trouble!

Just out of curiosity, I asked this billing officer what the terms of the loan were. She answered: "Seven point eight percent." I burst out laughing and asked her: "Can *you* get nearly 8 percent on your money anywhere right now?" She chuckled, paused, and said, "Are you kidding?" I immediately called my daughter and explained what had just happened. I informed her that I could get a home equity line or a mortgage for close to 3 percent, but the student loan industry was attempting to charge us 8 percent to borrow from them, and practically insisting that we take their money. It was a great object lesson and allowed me to personally experience what I have been preaching against for years. Student loans are obviously a very easy trap to fall into, even for the alert.

The costs of the loan payback are fixed and guaranteed (unless you miss a payment, in which case they will go up) while the payoff for the college degree is largely unknown for most students. The typical high school graduate has nothing more than sheer speculation and optimism to guide his post-college earning expectations.

Fresh out of high school, student loans also provide a ready entry into a lifetime of a Buy Now-Pay Later consumer mentality. And, unlike other forms of debt, walking away will likely prove impossible. Consumers with excessive credit card debt may be able to have their debt discharged in bankruptcy or a negotiated settlement. Individuals who cannot pay their mortgages can return the house, and the debt, through foreclosure. Unfortunately, it is much harder to get out from under student loan debt. Student loans, according to the 2005 bankruptcy law, are almost impossible to escape. One reason for this harsh stipulation is because without it, a college student could simply declare bankruptcy the minute he graduates. The new "pay as you earn" student loan repayment plan has eligibility restrictions and only applies to federal student loans; don't let this highly touted program lull you into a state of complacency regarding debt.

Student debt can conceivably follow a student well into middle age. Unlike a thirty-year mortgage or a car loan, you can't sell your asset (your education) or turn in the keys to walk away. That's because your life is the asset that backs the loan. Therefore, student loans should always be approached in a spirit of seriousness and with utmost caution. Whenever possible, avoid them. It is also worth remembering that when you take on student loans, in most cases you are dealing with the Feds. The federal government is far less forgiving and far more formidable than any private bank, with far greater resources at its disposal to track down debtors.

CAUTION: APPROACHING COLLEGE DEBT

Okay, okay, you get the idea. Student loans are risky, they are larger than ever, and they are piling up on unsuspecting, trusting college students. What can you do about them? The answer is plenty, but it has to be done before you go into debt in the first place!

You must be ruthlessly realistic about what you can afford to pay for college. Many high school students have very little understanding of the world of credit and its repercussions and responsibility—understandably, since up to this point they haven't had to deal with it. Parents have to take the lead in providing safe boundaries.

The first step in maintaining safe loan boundaries is to face your financial limits. One way to do this is to write down exactly how much money you will be able to contribute to college education. Place the number here, in black and white, knowing that you need to commit to that.

$ _____

You probably feel startled by such a blunt request. Certainly, college financial aid officers will never be this forthright with you. Instead, they will tell you how the college is going to "work with you" to find an affordable way to "finance" college. This mushy approach is far more dangerous. Blunt is good, because it forces you to face facts and be brutally honest about what you are actually able to afford.

If you don't know where to begin, a good place to start is by listing the amount of money you have already set aside for college. (If you haven't set aside much, or anything, you are not alone. *Money* magazine reports that the average family of a teenager in America has set aside less than $7,000 for college.) Next, add to this the amount of money you will be able to spare from your salary over the next four years.

Please be levelheaded in assessing how much you can reasonably afford to pay for college. Don't jeopardize your retirement or plan to scale back your standard of living to ramen noodle levels just so your child can attend a particular name-brand school. Status colleges are not necessary for achieving career aspirations, and an individual's life chances will not be harmed by financial prudence. Quite the contrary, really. Financial restraint now can mean more opportunities for your child later.

It is perfectly all right if the number you write down is not large. The important thing is to put the number down in black and white so that you are being completely honest about what you are able to pay for schooling after high school. This base commitment will determine the parameters that will drive the rest of your college planning. Parents should share this number with their child and use it, together, to make smart college choices.

START WITH YOUR PROJECTED EARNINGS

Now, let's review New Reality Rule 14: Base your college borrowing on your expected entry-level earnings. One variant of this rule is this: Don't borrow more in four years than your starting salary at graduation. If a student is going to college to become a teacher, then a little research shows he can expect to earn about $35,000 in the first year of work. It follows, then, that a student cannot afford to borrow more than $8,750 for each year of college, for a total of the entire starting salary. More than that, and he probably will not earn enough money to make the monthly payments. This is a rough estimate, but it is a good working number that provides helpful parameters to prevent costly overreaching.

Now, parents may be thinking: But my child doesn't know what he wants to do for a major or a career yet. That's why I'm sending him to college! If that is your perspective, then you are entering very risky waters. A student who goes to college without any clear career goals, and borrows money to pay for it, is heaping mistake upon mistake. Without any idea of how much he might earn, how can he possibly judge how much he can comfortably afford to borrow? The answer, of course, is that he can't. These undecided students are the most likely to borrow unrealistic amounts and wind up in trouble.

Students without clear career goals are also more likely to drop out of college, thereby compounding their economic problems. They are more likely to switch majors or transfer schools, a decision which typically adds at least one year to the length of time it takes to graduate and inflates the cost. Incidentally, 60 percent of college students now change majors or transfer at some point. Is it any wonder we have a student debt crisis?

To effectively follow the new rule of college loans, a student must do enough career planning to be able to estimate his future earning potential. This rough accounting forces the issue and makes it clear to the student that the investment in college is meant to yield a dividend on the other side.

If you're a student undecided on your major, and *if* you're lucky enough to find a job right after graduation—an optimistic assumption in itself—you can probably expect to earn around $40,000. You should borrow no more than $40,000 in student loans total, which means going no more than $10,000 in debt per year. Using this starting salary as an example, you can then begin to anticipate what your post-college budget will look like.

SAMPLE SALARIES

You can find some sample starting salaries at *www.salary .com*. Here are some typical ones:

Accountant	$33,000
Accounting Manager	$83,000
Engineer	$50,000
Nurse	$50,000
Nurse Practioner	$90,000
Paralegal	$47,000
Teacher	$35,000

Let's look at a simplified after-college budget for this hypothetical student. After taxes, a student making $40,000 can expect to bring home about $3,000 a month. From that amount, the student may expect to pay about $1,000 a month for housing, $350 a month for a car payment and gas, $400 a month for food, and he would have a $460 a month student loan payment. That is assuming the loan is at 6.8 percent amortized over ten years. This leaves less than $800 a month for everything else, and the student still hasn't paid for a cell phone, cable TV, or Internet connection, yet! It also doesn't include any health-care bills or insurance premiums. That's a pretty tight budget.

This exercise can help to open everyone's eyes to the challenges the student and his family will face by taking on loans that are too large to comfortably repay. Parents, you might ask a college-bound student how he would feel about living in his childhood room for a few years after college. Students, you might ask your parents the same thing. That may help pound the truth about borrowing limits home.

Parents, you should be prepared to help your child think things through when it comes to assuming student loans. Underage children and teenagers are prevented by law from entering into agreements or other commitments that they cannot understand or fulfill. Normally, a minor cannot be held liable for any contract he might sign and such an agreement would automatically be considered void. Believe it or not, *one of the only exceptions to this prudent law is student loans.* The government actually makes a legal exception to the defense of infancy for the assumption of federal student loans, and several states have followed suit in passing similar laws to consider minors to be competent for the purpose of assuming a loan for educational purposes.

CALCULATE YOUR FUTURE SALARY

Want a more accurate estimate of a college student's future earning capacity? Visit *www.humancapital score.com* for a personalized prediction of likely earning prospects. This nifty site calculates earning potential using such factors as GPA, standardized test scores, college and major. This tool is sure to provide an enormous wake-up call for many future literature and sociology majors! Why deal in guesstimates when you can access cold, hard data to convince a student of his repayment limits? This site provides reliable evidence to guide your decision-making and expectations.

DON'T EXPECT THE COLLEGE TO HELP

Finally, don't ever expect a college to tell you that a student can't afford to go there. This is simply not going to happen. It is not in the school's interest to deliver that crushing news. You have to make that determination yourself. Every college will tell you that it has ways (loans) of making the school affordable to you and that the sacrifices are worth it. You have to exercise restraint and discuss it as a family. Even though it may be hard to make the decision not to go to the first school of choice, you'll be much happier when you are not drowning in debt like many of your well-intentioned but misguided friends.

REALITY RULE #15

OLD RULE:	NEW RULE:
Save money for college.	*Savers are penalized by the financial aid system. Shelter money instead.*

It makes good logical sense to think that when you are facing a large upcoming financial expenditure, such as college, you should begin saving for it in advance. It's only logical, plus it's the responsible thing to do to try to avoid debt. This is the way prior generations used to think about buying a house, or a car, or even something as simple as a washing machine.

The trouble with thinking this way is that you are not thinking the way the people who wrote the financial aid formula think. Unfortunately, the financial aid formula punishes families for exercising such financial prudence. It does so by raising the amount savers are expected to pay for college.

Zac Bissonnette, the author of *Debt-Free U*, delightfully tagged the federal FAFSA form as standing for a "Federal Assault on Family Savings Accounts." This isn't far off the mark. The formula has declared open season on your savings and checking accounts. The more you save, the more you will be asked to pay for college. Remember that the FAFSA form and the financial aid formula focus on your existing assets. Their assumption is that if you've got money in a savings account, you clearly won't need much financial aid—even if that savings account has been earmarked for other purposes.

The financial aid formula is rife with moral hazard and perverse incentives. It punishes good behavior, such as thrift, and rewards you for failing to plan financially for college or for spending all of your money. There is no financial aid penalty for being a spendthrift or for living in a home you cannot afford. Instead, the formula will subsidize you for doing so by lowering your expected contribution. Families who live beyond their means receive a bonus, and families who sacrifice to live below their means, and set money aside, get to pay extra.

Therefore, it is quite possible for a student to show up on a college campus and be handed a bill for the entire amount of tuition while attending classes with students from more affluent families who live in bigger homes—and who are receiving financial aid. Consider it a tax on you for being thrifty. The FAFSA only looks at the assets you have or don't have; the formula doesn't consider how hard you worked or how much you scrimped or sacrificed to accumulate them. There are no points for effort.

Imagine two identical, hypothetical families. Both are earning $120,000 a year. One lives in a large home that cost over $400,000 and drives a new Lexus. They trade in their luxury car every two years and take several vacations per year. They eat out regularly. They have no money set aside for college and nothing in savings. Instead, they are in debt. They just bought their beautiful new home, so they have no equity. Their child has never worked a job and spent every dollar he received for birthdays and holidays over the years. They deny themselves nothing.

The other family lives in a more modest ranch house that cost them $200,000. They have never moved and made extra payments to pay off their mortgage. They rarely eat out or vacation, and so they have responsibly managed to set aside $200,000 in savings accounts for college. Of course, they are still anxious, because this is still not quite enough to pay the entire cost of attendance at some private colleges, and they have two college-bound children. Their oldest child has worked since age sixteen and has managed to set aside an impressive $10,000 for college out of his own earnings. His parents taught him to save and invest all the monetary gifts he received over the years for another $10,000 in savings—$20,000 total. Last year, in preparation for college, he earned $5,000 mowing lawns and working at McDonalds.

The first family, living large, will be expected to pay $29,593 each year for college, while the thrifty family will be charged $43,187 per year. You read that right. Hence, their savings cost them $13,594 each year, for a total additional cost of $54,376 over four years. That is their savings penalty—the amount they would *not* have been charged if they had been *less* responsible with their money. This additional cost is more than a quarter of their entire life savings. If they had spent this money instead on a bigger home, vacations, or other consumption costs, they could have received that money in financial aid. (Readers, please note here that I'm *not* urging you down a path of fiscal irresponsibility. The solution to the financial aid problem is not to live beyond your means.)

At a private college that uses the PROFILE form to determine aid eligibility, the second family would be expected to pay a whopping $54,467 per year, mainly due to their home equity, which this formula considers. The family with no savings or equity would be charged an additional $1,000, for a total of $30,593. This means the family with savings and equity could be charged $24,000 more annually at a private college. This adds up to a total additional savings penalty over four years of $95,000, or nearly *half* of their total life savings.

Was their thrift worth it? If this same family had sacrificed nothing and spent all their money instead, they would have been asked to pay far less for college. The thrifty family will avoid some loans, but they could have spent the extra money they were charged on a boat, new cars, a vacation home, jewelry, or any number of personal possessions that they would get to keep and enjoy after college is over. Should they just spend that money instead, rather than having additional costs added onto their tuition bills? It's a compelling possibility to consider. If they didn't have the savings, they wouldn't be asked to turn it over, and they sacrificed more than the other family to accumulate it by living frugally. Where is the fairness in this? You can see why I am not a fan of the existing financial aid system.

To rub salt in the wounds, one way in which the family that failed to save is offered financial aid is through the transfer of some of the tuition dollars collected from the thrifty family who is being charged a higher price to attend. Money from full-pay families is used by many institutions to help provide grants to other students who qualify for aid. In essence, the system rewards irresponsible behavior and punishes thrift.

What if the thrifty family had saved their $200,000 in the child's name, since they were planning to use it to pay for college? This would be a huge mistake: The family's expected contribution would then soar to over $50,000, and they would not qualify for any aid. Because the formula assumes that the student doesn't really need the money in his name, it will add 20–25 percent of the total amount to each year's tuition costs. All because the family switched how those assets were held.

VICTIMIZED BY THE SYSTEM

The point is this: Those who do not understand the financial aid system can be unfairly victimized by it. At today's tuition price levels, families cannot afford to be ignorant of the existing system and its various incentives and disincentives. The current formula includes an enormous marriage penalty. Divorced families can effectively cut their income in half. The formula only counts the income of the custodial parent. The other parent's income is ignored. The formula punishes students for working hard to contribute to the cost of their own education, and it makes saving for college counterproductive for many families.

The wise family will focus on learning the various components of the FAFSA formula and shelter their money from it, legally. Some nonassessed vehicles for doing so include life insurance and retirement accounts. Savings, checking, and even 529 accounts, unfortunately, are all assessed. In consultation with your financial adviser, you need to find the best vehicles for sheltering your money in order to maximize the amount of financial aid for which you will qualify.

REALITY RULE #16

OLD RULE:	NEW RULE:
There is nothing you can do about high tuition.	*Everything is negotiable, from tuition to how long it takes to graduate.*

Most families feel as though they are at the mercy of listed tuition rates and consider the pricing fixed. The majority of families with college-bound students spend far more time obsessing over how they will gain admission to college than figuring out how they will manage to pay for it. In fact, the college admissions process seems deliberately set up to support this skewed emphasis, since it precedes the financial aid award and negotiation process. By the time students have completed their applications, they and their supportive families have little energy or enthusiasm left for this final stage.

Anyone who has ever dealt with a skilled salesperson knows that the way to make a sale is first to build a strong desire for the product. Once the consumer has made an emotional commitment to purchase a product, pricing becomes a secondary consideration. I suspect that this is why the financial aid part of the college application comes last.

For a typical middle-class family, college may turn out to be the most complicated purchase of their lives. Our typical consumer habits, such as saving up to make a big down payment on a car or home, can backfire when applied to college planning, due to the baffling mysteries of financial aid and the penalty applied against savers. As students march through the application process senior year, a sense of inevitability and inescapability seems to overtake families. The peer pressure is intense—both for parents and students! It is understandably difficult to place limits on your child's college options when most of his peers are being told that the postsecondary educational world is their oyster. It's equally hard, if you're a student, to see your friends leave for great schools when you're desperately wondering how you're going to pay for your tuition and board. Often the only reasonable option for both parents and students seems to be to bite the bullet and pay. For most families, this means taking on debt.

Consider the Alternatives

In reality, there are all sorts of options. First of all, don't assume that tuition prices are written in stone. They are not. Discounts are given to many students, and there is probably a school that will offer your family a discount, too, if you are willing to be flexible in your postsecondary options. The reason schools offer tuition discounts to some students is precisely to entice them to attend. Listen to these offers and consider them seriously. It might not be your first choice of schools, but that is why they are making the offer: to try to get your attention and encourage you to reconsider. They want to make you a deal. Be open to what schools offering discounts have to say. Being flexible can really pay off.

There are also many ways to earn a bachelor's degree. It's like planning a journey. If I want to visit Rome, for instance, I know that there are several ways to make it happen.

- **I could fly first-class during peak travel times, stay at the most expensive hotel, and linger there for months.**

- **More likely, since money is a consideration, I will buy my plane ticket early, sit in the tight seats, travel off-peak, book reservations at a moderately priced hotel, and limit the length of my stay to reduce my costs.**

The same principle applies to college; there are wildly expensive options and there are more affordable options. If money is a concern, you will want to plan creatively and take advantage of the most economical choices. Either way, you can still reach the same destination.

When it comes to airplane travel, those who book early normally receive the best tickets. When it comes to college, it works the opposite way. Those who book early, by making an early decision, often pay a premium. This is because those early applicants have shown their hand. They have essentially told the college that the student definitely plans to attend, before they've even heard the details of the financial aid offer. It is the college equivalent of shopping for houses, finding your dream home, spinning in a circle in the living room with your arms outstretched, and announcing to the realtor: "I'll *take* it! I *have* to have this house, no matter *what*!" Obviously, in both the case of the realtor and the college, the seller knows he won't have to lower the price to close the deal.

Those who book late for college (which in this case means by applying with the regular admissions pool) may gain better price concessions. You may receive steeper discounts, because the colleges know that you may have other compelling offers of admission and they have to compete to get you to commit to their school. It's similar to a car salesman trying to meet his sales quota at the end of the month. The level of deal he may offer a potential buyer depends largely on how badly he wants to make the sale. Zac Bissonnette, the author of *Debt-Free U*, refers to those who "sell" college as "college dealers," which is not far off. There is definitely some wheeling and dealing going on.

This financial aid disadvantage is one of the ways in which early admissions programs subtly discriminate against the middle classes and favor the wealthy, who don't have to worry about financial aid packages to finance their attendance. Those who are price sensitive can't afford to give up their option to compare aid packages. This implicit bias is why Harvard and a few other select schools discontinued the practice on a trial basis. Interestingly enough, after a brief hiatus, Harvard has already decided to revive early admissions.

Look for Discounts

Remember: At most colleges, tuition prices are not immutably fixed. Many families receive tuition discounts, and you should expect one, too, given the exorbitant prices most colleges now charge. Discounts come in many forms: Scholarships, grants, and generous need-based aid packages are some of the most common. At some schools, nearly every student receives at least a nominal discount of, say, $1,500 just to take some of the sting out of the sticker price.

Without belaboring the car-buying analogy too much, this is a very useful metaphor for understanding why a family must never pay retail for a college degree. The sticker price of a car is inflated to allow some wiggle room for negotiation. Therefore, every car buyer expects, and generally receives, a discount in the purchase price of the vehicle. Colleges—particularly the expensive private ones—deliberately set tuition prices high to extract as much money as possible from the full-pay families who do not qualify for any need-based financial aid. This is hardly a secret; I have heard administrators readily admit to this fact, while acknowledging that the extra amounts the full-pays spend allow the college to admit and fund other students who receive substantial discounts. In "The Prestige Racket," an article in the *Washington Monthly*, writer Daniel Luzer uses George Washington University to highlight this fiscal strategy. The college, he says, "uses rich kids to subsidize the education of poor kids—an argument that is common among the leaders of private universities that charge high tuition." Pointing out that 40 percent of students at GWU pay the full list price, Luzer quotes the former president Stephen Trachtenberg's view justifying its exorbitance: "These are people from wealthy families; I have no compunction about charging them list price. They can afford it."

It may be true that wealthy families can afford the higher tuition. For those middle-class families who just barely fall into the full-pay category, though, this is an extraordinarily bad deal.

Give Yourself a Scholarship

You don't have to be an alma martyr and sacrifice your financial future on the altar of outrageous college costs. After utilizing every strategy to maximize your financial aid eligibility, if the price is still too high, you can always do something I call: "Give yourself a scholarship." Accumulate free or low-cost college credits during high school. You can take extra credits each semester to speed the time to graduation by putting in more study effort. You can use the two-year transfer option, by starting off at a lower-priced school and then transferring into your dream college. If transferring is not for you, what about taking cheap summer courses at the local community college and transferring them to your main college? Many schools will allow you to transfer in a certain number of credits this way. It is the same principle as studying abroad, where you take courses at a foreign university and the home college accepts the credit. Some schools call it "Domestic Study Abroad," and you can save thousands of dollars this way. You must do your homework, however, to make sure that all the courses you take will be accepted.

Be Flexible about School Choice

You know what else is always negotiable? Attendance at a particular school. It has never been more important for middle-class families, in particular, to insist upon affordable colleges with demonstrable results. Colleges have to be able to show that graduates obtain employment in order to justify the prices they charge. Just as with any other financial negotiation, walking away is always on the table, and enrollment, just because a student is admitted, is never a foregone conclusion. A bad deal is a bad deal and should be refused. Fortunately, American college students have multiple postsecondary options available to them, in every price range.

PART III

ENTERING THE REAL WORLD

Quo vadis?

Today's college graduates are struggling to enter the workforce. After spending vastly higher sums for their educations, they simply can't expect the plentiful job offers that previous generations of diploma-bearers received after commencement. Therefore, this last section focuses on new ideas for helping graduates to make the transition to employment, despite the increase in competition. After all, that is probably the most cherished, if unstated, expectation of every parent and college-bound student—that afterward, the student will be able to find a good job.

It used to be enough for a high school student to simply say, "I'm going to college." That, in itself, was once regarded as a sufficient—even impressive—career decision with a guaranteed bright future. No more. To beat the odds in finding gainful employment, young people must equip themselves with more than just a sheepskin. They are also going to need to adopt fresh attitudes and assume new responsibilities. They must approach college more deliberately and make better use of their opportunities once there. This is the only way to stand out from plentiful other job applicants. Admittedly, this is a very tall order for a young graduate, so parents must stay involved and offer practical help along the way. After all, this concerns the parents' future financial well-being as well as the child's!

CHAPTER 8

TARGETING YOUR DEGREE TO THE JOB MARKET

REALITY RULE #17

OLD RULE:	NEW RULE:
Liberal arts graduates can do "anything."	*Make sure your degree has a clear relation to existing or emerging jobs.*

liberal arts education, according to the conventional wisdom, can take you anywhere you want to go in life. Because you are broadly educated, the wisdom goes, you will be able to rise as high as you want. The problem with a liberal arts major is finding a clear relationship between, say, a college degree in history and existing job openings. One president of a local temporary agency recently informed me that, he could "probably" find a job for a history or English major . . . at $9 an hour. Good luck paying off your student loans or moving out of your parents' house at that rate!

The pendulum among those involved in the education and career fields swings back and forth between recommending a liberal arts degree and a more career-oriented educational program. When the economy is strong and job opportunities are plentiful, people tend to favor liberal arts education with its broad exposure to many areas of inquiry and unlimited potential. When economic times are bad, the advice tends to swing in the other direction, toward more focused vocational training, which includes fields requiring licensure or certification beyond a diploma. These programs offer more specific career training with a clearer relationship to existing jobs in the labor market. They also limit competition, because those without the required credential are not eligible to apply for open positions.

Examples of licensure and certification requirements include teaching certificates, CPA credentials, nursing registration, and even the bar exam for lawyers and medical qualifying examination for doctors, both of which are required by states to begin a practice. Essentially, these careers are closed shops. You cannot enter without the right piece of paper.

WHAT CAN YOU AFFORD?

These days, it makes a great deal of sense to earn a certification or licensure *in addition to* a liberal arts degree. If you really want to be an English major, fine. That's what I did. But, as I mentioned earlier, I graduated into the recession that followed the stock market crash of 1987, and I was born at the tail end of the baby boom. I entered a workforce that was already saturated with elders who had more experience than I possessed. My first job offer, from a major Manhattan publishing house, came with a salary that amounted to $6.50 an hour—less than I had made waiting tables during high school, only now I possessed an Ivy League degree. Even though the publishing offer was an exciting job, I had to turn it down because I couldn't afford to take it.

Even worse, I would scan the want ads in my hometown and see multiple positions for dental hygienists paying $25 an hour. Some even offered hiring bonuses because trained hygienists were in such high demand! Twenty-five dollars an hour seemed like a princely sum to me back in the 1980s, and most people wouldn't turn their noses up at that wage today. I was horrified to realize that I wasn't qualified to support myself while two-year graduates were. I took a little bit of time to nurse my injuries, but then I quickly faced the fact that the market decides what labor is worth. I also remembered the button slogans that union laborers wore at Harvard when they were fighting for higher wages. The buttons read: "You can't eat prestige." I took that message to heart, swallowed my pride, and got serious about earning a credential that would enable me to make a better wage than what I had been offered so far.

Luckily, at the time, New Jersey was offering "Alternate Route" public school teaching certification to encourage graduates of liberal arts colleges to become educators. I took advantage of this opportunity and have been in education in some form or another ever since. This is yet another reason why I am such a believer in the value of possessing licensure credentials. They have proven, measurable, and enduring value in the marketplace, whereas the bachelor's degree's value is declining. If being self-supporting as soon as possible after college is a priority, look into career-linked majors and licensure or certification opportunities.

Many students also need to learn that they will have to focus on the needs of others, rather than on their own personal desires, to find economic success. It is very common to think, "If I am smart and well educated, people will want to hire me." There may be some truth to this, but employers (like everyone else) are selfish. They only want to hire smart people who can understand that they are there to meet the organization's needs—not their own. Employers have to see what's in the hiring bargain for them. The sooner this lesson sinks in, the faster a student will understand how to position himself for success and market himself effectively. Both college admissions and job hunting require a keen focus on the needs of the audience, rather than on the desires of the applicant.

What Do Employers Want?

The average college student needs to think less about what he is interested in and more about what other people are willing to pay for. No, it's not idealistic, but this is a sobering wake-up call most of us eventually encounter in adulthood, anyway. Better to learn it while there is still time to switch a college major to something with brighter prospects than to spend a small fortune on a degree with little value and be left without enough money to pursue retraining or shift gears. What does the current economy require? What do people need? There is really nothing more satisfying, or potentially lucrative, than helping other people get what they want.

The student who can focus on recognizing, anticipating, and meeting existing or developing needs in the larger economy will find the greatest success. College is supposed to teach students to collect information, analyze it, and then come to intelligent conclusions. Let's apply those abilities to the workforce. What do we know about the economy? Well, we know that there are a lot of unemployed people—the most we've seen in a long time, with particularly high unemployment rates for teens and young adults. We also know that we are facing some major demographic shifts. Demography is often a very reliable indicator of long-term future trends, since the economy can change suddenly due to unanticipated events, but aging is predictable.

If you examine the chart below, you will see that the American demographic profile is no longer shaped like a pyramid, with a small number of old people on top and much larger numbers of younger people in the middle and at the bottom.

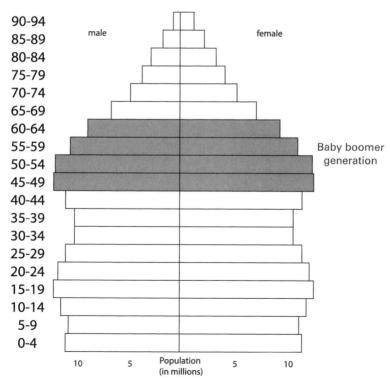

United States Population in 2010

Instead, the current demographic chart appears to have developed a waist and hips. The highlighted bulge near the top of this chart depicts the baby boomer generation, which still holds a significant number of jobs in the economy and is reluctant to shift into retirement. This large generation continues to overshadow those who follow it in the workforce and will continue to be influential for decades. This is enormously significant, and I should point out how unprecedented in human history it is to have larger numbers of older people than younger people in a population. Ages ago, the only reasons for this to happen would be wars, famine, or pestilence. Today contraception is reducing the birthrate, and medical science is extending our lifespan. We have never experienced this situation before and it has enormous implications for our economy and for younger generations.

Presumably, as these boomers age, they should fuel growing demands for all the goods and services typically consumed by the elderly, including health care and also, for the newly retired active adults, entertainment and travel. We can conclude that there should be a growing need for health-care administration as well as audiology and optometry services for those losing their hearing and eyesight. The frail elderly may require home aids, for assistance with daily living. Home care is not typically a college-level job, but perhaps an enterprising college graduate could start a business focused on supplying this need? Even morticians can expect to see plentiful business in coming years. It is only logical. The way to succeed in business is always to see emerging opportunities and prepare to take advantage of them.

Given the prolific character of young people coming of childbearing age, there will be a steady supply of children in coming years who will need to be educated. Thus teaching certification remains a good long-term bet, as job projections continue to indicate. Currently, education is a very top-heavy field, with large numbers of aging teachers and professors. Their impending retirements should create a wide range of education-oriented openings in the future. Of course, technology could impact how education is delivered in the future, making online education a field to consider.

America is also witnessing a great wave of immigration. What about teaching English as a second language to new inhabitants of the country? Computers have become indispensible commodities, making technology careers a fairly safe bet. (Just yesterday, I was walking through New York City and spotted an enormous billboard near Times Square that read: Do you know Linux? We're hiring!) Even criminal science is considered a growth field, due to the fact that America has such a high proportion of incarcerated citizens.

The point is that career plans should be based more on concrete facts and data than on wishful thinking and current, possibly fleeting, interests. A student who is able to survive economic downturns and find work even during a recession will be best positioned to survive occasional hard times and thrive as the economy improves.

Hopefully, as aging baby boomers slowly shift into retirement we will see a return to plentiful employment opportunities for young people. This demographic shift should move us from a labor surplus to a labor shortage, but it is going to take time—decades, in fact. In the meantime, students will have to work with present economic realities and demographic facts to find a welcoming place in the workforce.

In an era when so many young people are going to college, and the job market is so tight, undergraduates need to do anything and everything possible to position themselves for success when they enter the job market. From the employer's perspective, there are many college-educated applicants to choose from, so they will naturally be looking for obvious relationships between what an applicant studied and the jobs they have to offer. According to Certified Executive Coach Cheryl Jacobs, "Right now employers are focused on finding people who can hit the ground running. To get hired, you need to be able to demonstrate some kind of specialized knowledge." The right college degree assures employers that you have the expertise they want, which is particularly important for those new to the workforce or looking to transition careers.

Likewise, students with a defined interest in working for specific companies should do everything possible to secure advanced placement in their target firms. Make sure they know who you are. This means proactively seeking out informational interviews, creating job shadowing opportunities, and pursuing internships with them during college. It means networking and building connections to current employees and supervisors with decision-making authority.

The Internet makes networking easier than ever, since most industry insiders have a public presence and published contact information. In *Debt-Free U*, Zac Bissonnette advises all college students to boldly seek out influential individuals in their fields of interest. According to Bissonnette, the best career advice is, "Send e-mails to people you respect and admire. You never know what will come of it." He should know: As a high school student he wrote to his favorite financial writer and made a favorable impression. This led to an encounter at a fundraiser in New York, where he was seated next to a well-known literary agent and pitched his successful book idea. Bissonnette's story should inspire college students to tap into the power of networking and reach out to influential people.

REALITY RULE #18

OLD RULE:	NEW RULE:
The name of your undergraduate college is very important.	*Your last degree is what matters most.*

More college students are considering graduate school as a way of attaining the level of economic security that was once expected for college graduates. This is partly a cause and partly a result of ongoing credential inflation in the general economy. Pursuing this lengthy educational path is costly, both in terms of time and money.

Students who plan to attend graduate or professional school need to reserve funds for the long educational haul. It helps to remember that the name of their baccalaureate institution will matter less than the school from which their final degree is earned. Therefore, it might be advisable to attend a relatively inexpensive school—even without much prestige—for undergraduate work, and concentrate on getting into a prominent graduate program. The planning process for those going on to graduate programs is different, because college is only an intermediate step in the process.

THE VALUE OF GRADUATE SCHOOL

Many high school students embarking upon a college education do not understand much about graduate school and are unsure if they may want to attend at some point in the future.

So they approach college with a shorter-term view than a student who is firmly set on attending, say, medical school. Many, probably the majority, of high school students and a good many of their parents do not even understand the difference between a *college* and a *university*. It is no wonder they are confused; there is a great deal of fuzziness in how these terms are applied and used.

Generally speaking, a college focuses only on undergraduate teaching (the four years after high school). Colleges tend to be smaller than universities, and they normally do not offer any graduate programs. Colleges become universities when they add graduate-level programming.

Even something as simple as offering one master's degree program in education can be enough to trigger a name change from college to university. Colleges often like to assume the name *university* as soon as they qualify, since it can make them seem larger and more impressive. Universities tend to be bigger and better known than colleges. The most prestigious subset within the category of universities is the so-called *research university*. Research universities offer doctoral degrees and typically engage in sophisticated advanced studies, often with support from the federal government or foundations. As such, they often have access to substantial resources and equipment. Research universities include some of the biggest names in higher education, including Harvard, Yale, Princeton, Stanford, and Johns Hopkins. These are the prestigious schools that attract attention and competition for admission.

What Does an Undergraduate Really Need?

The reason I bring up this whole discussion of colleges versus universities is because the difference is relevant to the selection process in high school. If a student is planning to go to medical school, or to obtain a PhD, then he or she will eventually need to wind up at a university for the doctorate degree. At the undergraduate level, however, much of what characterizes or distinguishes a large university may be largely irrelevant or superfluous. Does an undergraduate student really need access to an electron microscope? A college library with more than 3 million books in it? To sit in a lecture hall with a Nobel Laureate as opposed to an ordinary professor?

Maybe. Then again, probably not. Many of the resources that admissions offices like to brag about and point out on tours are really unnecessary and likely inaccessible for a typical—or even an advanced—undergraduate student.

For instance, driving through Penn State's campus not long ago, I noticed a sign on a building for their nuclear reactor. Now, I admittedly don't know much about nuclear energy, but it is a safe bet that this facility exists mainly for research by graduate students and professors. I suppose it's possible that the undergraduates may be able to tour it, or even see a demonstration of it, but I would be very surprised (and a little bit frightened) if any of them get to operate it. They have too many fundamental courses and topics to cover before they need such a rare and specialized piece of equipment.

These are the sorts of resources needed by a student pursuing a PhD in nuclear engineering, however. The same goes for aspiring doctoral students in any field, who will want to look very closely at the specific resources available in graduate schools in their areas of specialization. For the typical undergraduate student at Penn State, though, that reactor may as well not even be there. Most undergraduate students will never take advantage of any of these highly specialized resources and, if they do manage to sit in a class taught by a Nobel Laureate, they will likely only be interacting with and graded by one of his graduate students in the breakout teaching sections. Direct access to the highest-level professors in elite universities is usually reserved for graduate-level students.

In other words, at a major university, you might be paying for access to a lot of things you don't really need at the undergraduate level and might not even be allowed to use. They look impressive and sound nice, but are they really contributing substantively to your education? There are only so many volumes an undergraduate can read in four years; does the average student need access to mega-millions of books? Why pay extra for resources you will not use?

Access to Professors

Teaching access is another important part of the crucial difference between a major research university and a smaller college. At a liberal arts college, the professors may not have the same level of name recognition, but the students will have closer contact with them. In between are the smaller, less prestigious universities, including many second-tier state schools, some of which still provide relatively small class sizes and easy access to faculty. But the schools that seem to attract the most attention and garner the greatest number of applications continue to be the big-name research universities where many resources will be of little direct value to those completing undergraduate degrees. Professors at these schools typically devote the majority of their attention to working with their graduate students and conducting research. These graduate students often assume a great deal of responsibility for helping to teach the undergraduate students.

A research university is supposed to be devoted to pushing forward the boundaries of knowledge through advanced, cutting-edge academic studies, but in order to reach that point, an undergraduate must first complete courses covering foundational knowledge. This basic work is necessary before a student can comprehend—much less participate in—more sophisticated research projects. (Students who are an exception to this at the undergraduate level will already know who you are.) For most college students, you can acquire this background knowledge effectively, at far less cost, at reasonably priced post-secondary institutions than at high-priced elite schools.

There is another practical reason to consider foregoing the elite research university option if you're planning on graduate school. The competition for grades is typically fiercer at these schools, which can actually make gaining admission to elite graduate schools more difficult. Many graduates of less prestigious undergraduate colleges routinely gain admission to top graduate schools, in part because many universities recognize that some of these smaller colleges actually do a better job of teaching the fundamentals than the big-name schools do!

Beware of Academic Inbreeding!

Also, there is something called *academic incest*. This means that major universities typically encourage their own bright undergrads to pursue graduate training elsewhere, in order to ensure that they are exposed to many different researchers and ideas. Fears of academic inbreeding cause many universities to limit the number of students who will be accepted from the undergraduate program into the graduate school at the same university. Therefore, if a student is interested in attending a particular graduate school, it can make sense to *avoid* the undergraduate program at the same institution. Exceptions do exist, so check with the graduate school admissions office to ask for their advice.

The theory of "satisficing" can help us realize that some things are unnecessary at the undergraduate level and will contribute little, if anything, to future success while adding enormously to the cost. When it is all said and done, the local, affordable public university may offer everything that is necessary to meet a student's baccalaureate needs. A bachelor's-level education should focus on mastering the existing status of knowledge in a field while gaining wide exposure to introductory levels of knowledge in a variety of core academic areas. This does not generally mandate access to the latest, most expensive technology at the cutting-edge fringes of research within a field. Often, undergraduate programs within a large university will even have one library devoted to serving just the undergraduates, because the more specialized resources found in graduate school libraries are unnecessary.

For these reasons, attending an elite university is more likely to be cost-effective at the graduate level than the undergraduate level. Undergraduates should be able to find what they need at less-expensive schools. The most important factors influencing graduate school admissions will be grades, graduate test scores, and letters of recommendation—not the name of the school. In fact, gaining meaningful letters of recommendation is typically harder at a big research university, because it is much more difficult to get to know professors personally. Impressive-sounding major research universities also typically have many more graduate students than undergraduates, leading you to wonder where their main allegiances lie and where most of their funding goes.

If a student is planning on going on to graduate school, the name of the last degree she earns is going to be far more important than the name of her undergraduate college. The bottom line is this: If you think that college is going to be your last degree, spend more on it. If you are pretty sure it's not, spend less, and reserve funds for graduate school.

REALITY RULE #19

OLD RULE:	NEW RULE:
A college degree is necessary for a middle-class lifestyle.	*A profession or skill in demand is necessary for a middle-class lifestyle.*

The connection between college and most careers has always been more vague than direct—a marriage of convenience. College degrees have served as a useful sorting tool and screening mechanism in the absence of other objective employment selection criteria. No one ever really assessed the validity of this college-centered screening process, but over time, it became standard practice. Through credential inflation, the bachelor's degree came to be seen as a requirement for many jobs that were once awarded to high school graduates.

BACHELOR'S DEGREE REQUIRED?

The employment situation for college graduates is now worsening, however, and the steady rise in the number of college graduates is a major contributing factor. There simply are not enough college-level jobs to absorb all of the hope-filled college-level graduates we are currently producing.

In some ways, a degree is passive; something you have. A skill, however, is something you can *do*. The degree is nice to have, but what will earn you a paycheck is your ability to perform some valuable activity that others cannot. Hopefully, students will gain high-wage skills in their college programs, but sometimes they do not. It is not terribly surprising, then, that some college graduates are now choosing to become skilled manual laborers, such as plumbers, welders, and electricians.

═COLLEGE BY THE NUMBERS═

According to workforce consultants and authors Kenneth Gray and Edwin Herr, just 21 percent of all jobs in the United States currently require a bachelor's degree or higher. There are now more than twice as many college graduates as there are jobs requiring this level of education. Clearly, a college degree alone is no safe haven in this seismic economic shift. Without skills in demand, many college graduates will fail to find satisfactory employment, or perhaps any employment at all.

═══════════════════ $ ═══════════════════

These graduates are choosing to become *reverse transfers,* meaning that they enroll in a community or technical college after earning their bachelor's degree, to develop more specialized skills. It can make sense, especially when you consider the high hourly wages these skilled workers can earn. Laurence Kotlikoff, a Boston University economist, recently demonstrated how a plumber can end up with virtually the same spending power as a doctor, when you add in his extra earning years and subtract out the cost of paying for medical school.

Overseas Competition

Another big advantage of a hands-on, skill-based career is that it is difficult to shift the labor to lower-paid workers overseas. Most people don't really think about it, but medicine is a hands-on profession. They cannot operate on your tumor in China or India any more than they can fix your air conditioner or cut your hair overseas. College students need to remember that anything that can be digitized can potentially be outsourced to cheaper foreign labor. This includes many types of college-level, computer-based knowledge labor. It means, unfortunately, office workers are at greater risk of losing their jobs to outsourcing than are dental hygienists.

The fact, welcome or not, is that job openings are determined by the demand for goods and services, rather than by the supply of workers. More college graduates will not lead to a higher demand for more college graduates by employers. Even the government's own workforce projections of the number of job openings in different career fields leave out a crucial element: the supply of qualified workers to fill them. This is precisely what will dictate the level of competition for available jobs, however. If this data were more widely available, then workers could make much more informed decisions about their educational and career plans.

High earnings are a reward for having skills that are in demand by people willing to pay for them. It's as simple as that. An employer looking at multiple applicants is going to hire the one with the skills most relevant to the business to avoid having to invest in more training. When everyone in the stack of applicants has a college degree, no one gains much competitive advantage from having one.

But What Can You *Do*?

Relating higher education to the workforce can be a hard concept for college students to grasp. I once attended a career session on "How to Get a Job in a Bad Economy" at a selective liberal arts college in the Northeast. This program was led by a very polished professional alumnus of the college and was targeted to anxious seniors who were still unemployed in late April, when the workshop was held. Clearly, these students were desperate. I sat in the back.

The presenter exhorted the eager students to activate their networks and put out the word that they were now available for hire. Then, he attempted to help them translate their coursework and extracurricular activities into concrete skills that employers might need. He pointed to student after student and asked them to use action words to describe practical skills they now possessed and could offer to a prospective employer. This was a stumper for all of them, and silence descended, until finally one female senior raised her hand. "Yes!" he thundered, expectantly. "Tell us one capability you have developed in college that employers need and will pay you for! Give me an action word!" Timidly, she responded: "Diversity?" At this, he was rendered speechless himself and quickly shifted to a new activity.

The point is that none of these students could express what it is they might actually be able to *do* to add value in the economic marketplace. Of course, their difficulty was not all their fault. College life has a way of insulating and isolating students from the real world to such an extent that multitudes of them have no earthly idea what goes on in an office building or how the majority of adults make a living.

Employers don't need employees who parrot the latest educational buzzwords and end their statements with a question mark, however. They need employees who can do things that fulfill real human needs and generate actual money. The only reason an employer will bother hiring anyone is if that person can bring in more money than they cost to hire. And, make no mistake: With the levels of student debt most new college graduates are going to be carrying, these students had better learn how to churn some cash . . . fast.

Employers need workers who can design, educate, analyze, compose, sell, gather, and interpret information, write code, and beat the competition to gain market share. They need people with good ideas, follow-through, a record of achievement, and the energy to get worthwhile things done. Even these vague statements need to be quantified and placed in a more specific context with evidence to back up any claims of possessing them. In the work world, *evidence* generally means *paid* work experience. Essentially, employers need reliable people who can prove that they know how to do things worth paying for!

A college degree alone isn't going to cut it, anymore. That much is clear. A degree will make a nice addition to whatever occupation a student intends to pursue, and it may help bring promotions down the line, but a student's initial career prospects now depend more on what he does beyond and outside the college degree than by anything else. The college degree is becoming a basic assumption that merely begs the question: But what can you actually *do*? A student needs to be able to answer that question concretely and convincingly.

To succeed today, and to achieve a reasonable middle-class lifestyle with a comfortable standard of living, students must acquire job skills that are in demand. You can locate some of the best available data on job demand and occupational outlooks at *www.careeronestop.org*. By entering the name of a certain career and clicking on "Outlook," you can see the exact number of jobs that the federal government anticipates in each different job category. You can also read details of the tasks associated with each position. When a student's abilities and preparation match with rising needs in the marketplace, he can find success.

Match Passions to Reality

There is much to be said for following one's passions in life. However, it can be a difficult, uphill battle when those passions are not in high demand or cannot command a living wage in the economic marketplace. College students can do themselves a big favor by being aware of current trends in the economy when choosing majors and making career plans.

One great way to gauge the realism of possible career options is for a student to test his ability to make money during college. A student studying something practical and in demand should be able to find paid employment or internships *in the field* before graduation. A student who is studying something impractical will not be able to find paid summer work in the field, and may have to rely on unrelated low-skill jobs to come up with spending cash. This should be seen as an early warning sign that the field of study may be in low demand in the marketplace.

The Down Side of Volunteerism

One of the most concerning economic signs I have noticed over the past few years is the incredible rise in unpaid opportunities for high school and college students. I believe that these have increased steadily as the number of actual, paying jobs has decreased. Many parents and students nowadays believe that community service opportunities will help set their students apart from the rest of an applicant pool and lead to a paying job later on. In my view, this hope is often largely misguided.

There are a number of reasons why I do not recommend unpaid, volunteer opportunities as a way of developing job skills or building a resume. Community service opportunities are plentiful and noncompetitive for one reason: They are almost always low-skill. They typically consist of very short assignments, lasting anywhere from a few hours to a few days, which can be completed by interchangeable spontaneous participants. They do not require the commitment of a real job. Normally, there are no required abilities or systematic on-the-job training.

Working a paying job, on the other hand, teaches a student his real worth in the actual economy and requires him to show up regularly or risk being fired. If a student can only command minimum wage in the labor force, then he has some feedback on what his skills are currently worth. This information may motivate him to aspire to something better.

Some students don't want to work for minimum wage or commit to spending their summer vacations bagging groceries. They would rather sign up for a summer community service trip in a far-off location. It is certainly more exciting to travel than it is to stay home and earn money, but the community service option keeps the student from participating in the economy. Having to work a crummy job can supply the motivation necessary for a student to begin developing higher-paying skills. The working student may look around and realize that the fellow sitting in the office doing the computer networking is earning ten times what he is making, without breaking a sweat. Suddenly, the student begins to appreciate the value of studying computer science.

A volunteer job teaches a student the exact opposite of that. It teaches him precisely what kinds of work people are *unwilling* to pay for. It actually trains him in working for free! This is not a sustainable lifetime habit. College students should become self-supporting as soon as possible; only then are they truly in a position to be able to donate their own time to a cause of their choosing.

WHAT'S BEHIND THE GROWTH OF VOLUNTEERISM?

My suspicion is that one of the unstated intentions of today's plentiful volunteer programs is to distract the younger generation from the limited employment opportunities available to them. I do not think that it is a coincidence that they seem to be proliferating as real job openings disappear. Even more amazingly, many colleges now have professional offices with salaried personnel devoted to finding unpaid experiences for students in the community. Often, these offices are much busier and better staffed than the career center! I cannot help but wonder what is stopping students from simply picking up the phone themselves and calling a local business or organization to ask if they could come and work there for free. Who would say "no" to that?

Because many community service opportunities take place far from home, a student (or, more likely, a student's family) is expected to pay the expense of transporting him to some distant site where his skills are presumably desperately required. Instead of earning money by working a paying job when he is not in class, the student is now consuming even more of the family's limited resources beyond tuition and room and board. I would characterize these types of opportunities under the category of "experiential travel," "enrichment activities," or "purchased experiences" rather than job experience, and employers (and admissions committees) are likely to feel the same way. They are looking for evidence of hard work and increasing responsibility, not for the ability to spend money.

Community service opportunities also serve to heighten the disparities between different economic classes in college. Many middle-class students, who receive limited to no aid, need to work jobs to help pay tuition. Wealthier students, and some lower-income students on generous aid packages, can afford to join nonpaying community service projects. Upon their return, they are likely to be featured in college newspapers with long articles, including pictures, extolling their selflessness. The middle-class student, who could not afford the plane ticket much less the time away from paid employment to participate in such adventures, is never praised for his hard work or sacrifice in contributing to his own economic support. I have yet to see a college newspaper feature a story about a student's hard work at an unglamorous summer job to earn money to pay tuition. The subliminal message to students is strong: Volunteer work is admired and paid work is ignored on campus. This is a very elitist view. It is different among employers, however. They value work experience.

Don't confuse unpaid volunteer experiences with a paying job. Real jobs pay real money. As for unpaid internships, my

: Entering the Real World

advice is to proceed with caution. Some top firms offer worth-while, unpaid internships; they are often quite prestigious and selective and can lead to job offers. But I still believe that the best internships are paid . . . or at the very least offer college credits for completion. Anything else comes dangerously close to exploitation.

The Importance of Internships . . . and Some Cautions

In high-demand fields, internships are paid in recognition of hard-to-find skills, so the presence of large numbers of unpaid internships should always raise concerns. In essence, it means that there is a larger supply of willing interns than there is demand for them. Ideally, an internship is brief and worthwhile, offering a potential employer the opportunity to try you out with low risk, or for a student to acquire supervised work skills that can be obtained no other way. At the very least, there should be some equitable *quid pro quo* for the student, even if it simply means receiving an impressive letter of recommendation or some course credits. However, when unemployed Harvard graduates are advertising their availability for unpaid internships, as is currently the case, something is clearly amiss.

I have always been skeptical of unpaid internships, and my suspicions were recently confirmed when I received an e-mail inviting me to a webinar where I, as a small business owner, could learn to "get free work from interns." If this isn't exploitation, I don't know what is. Rather than paying adults a fair wage, I should get desperate college students to work for me for nothing? I wondered why labor laws don't protect young people from this sort of treatment or why unions are not investigating and challenging unpaid internships. Workers with families to support are losing job opportunities to students willing to work for free . . . or, in reality, pay to work, since they presumably are being charged tuition while completing internships.

ACROSS THE POND

Internship problems are not confined to America. A recent article in a British newspaper describes similar unpaid exploitation of young people by media corporations, public relations agencies, and politicians (to name a few) in Great Britain, where the government is preparing to crack down on the practice. The article echoed my own conclusion: The only aspirants who can afford to work for free come from wealthy families that can afford to subsidize them, and so this expectation that newbies must initially labor for nothing effectively functions to keep middle- and lower-class young people from entering certain competitive, glamour fields.

Thankfully, there are finally new federal guidelines in place to counter decades of growing abuse of interns. The Department of Labor has stipulated legal criteria that now must be met for an internship to be offered unpaid, including the requirement that the internship be conducted for the training and educational benefit of the student—not merely to extract labor for free. In other words, a worthwhile internship offers a student the chance to learn something that will help her prepare for entry into a specific field that she could learn no other way. It should not be noneducational menial work. Of course, just because there are now better federal guidelines governing internships doesn't mean that enforcement will be perfect. Students will still have to scrutinize the opportunities they are offered.

The National Association of Colleges and Employers has proposed their own criteria for evaluating internships, which you can use to help measure the value of any internships you may be considering. According to NACE, an internship opportunity is legitimate when it is a learning experience of value to the intern. It should not simply be performing work that a regular employee would routinely do. The skills or knowledge learned must be transferable to other employment settings. The experience should have clearly defined learning objectives related to the professional goals of the intern, and the intern should receive supervision by an experienced professional with expertise in the field. The intern should also receive routine feedback from the supervisor and have access to resources, equipment, and facilities provided by the host employer that support the learning objectives and goals. In NACE's opinion, only an internship that meets all of these criteria should be offered unpaid. If you have found an unpaid internship opportunity that meets all these criteria, then this can be a great way to develop useful job skills and make valuable industry contacts. Otherwise, you deserve to be paid for your work.

When I graduated from college, the lowest rung on the employment ladder was temp work, with hourly wages but no benefits. This was the fallback career strategy for an applicant unable to secure a full-time position. Sure, it was demeaning, but at least it paid some bills while you continued your job search. Now, it appears companies in many fields are unwilling to pay even for that.

The bottom line is this: Don't get used to working for free. If it's work, you deserve to be paid for it and should expect nothing less.

I believe that it makes sense, in many avenues of life, to pursue a contrarian strategy and do something different from what the majority are doing. The sheer popularity of community service and other volunteer programs should in itself be an indication that this avenue is unlikely to set a student apart from the crowd in any meaningful way. If it seems like everyone is doing community service, then they will all list this on their resumes. If the majority of graduates are not finding jobs, this strategy of giving labor away for free is unlikely to work for you. If you want to do community service because you enjoy it, that's great . . . as long as you are supporting yourself and don't expect someone else to pay your bills while you do so. Otherwise, I believe students would be better off building their resumes by working paid jobs, even if they have to start at the very bottom rung of the employment ladder.

WHERE ARE THE JOBS GOING?

To avoid wandering into a field with poor career prospects, pay attention to general trends in the economy. The jobs in any economy always go where there are needs and money available to fill those needs. As the needs shift, the people who can best anticipate and meet emerging needs are positioned to profit the most.

Start with the Internet

For finding the latest statistics and information on careers, I recommend *www.careeronestop.org* and *www.onetonline.org*.

These government resources use statistics gathered by the United States Department of Labor and are as comprehensive as you will find anywhere. Here you will find information on careers, employment trends, salaries, growing and declining fields, job outlook, and education and training opportunities. Every college student should be familiar with these two career sites and research the job outlook and salary information on fields of interest thoroughly.

One of the most revealing searches you can conduct is to review careers with the most openings listed by education level. This gives you a good idea where there are likely to be opportunities in the future. I did a quick search of college-level occupations predicted to have the most job openings and got the following results:

1. **Elementary school teachers**

2. **Postsecondary (college) teachers**

3. **General and operations managers**

4. **Accountants and auditors**

5. **Secondary school teachers**

6. **Management analysts**

7. **Physicians and surgeons**

8. **Middle school teachers**

9. **Lawyers**

10. **Computer systems analysts**

11. **Computer software engineers applications**

12. **Clergy**

13. Network systems and data communications analysts

14. Computer software engineers, systems software

15. Financial managers

16. Construction managers

17. Market research analysts

18. Network and computer systems administrators

19. Public relations specialists

20. Securities, commodities, and financial services sales agent

Each of these occupations comes with a detailed description. Of course, this information changes regularly, so you will want to do an updated search of your own in order to access the most recent data. A college-bound student with no career direction may wish to focus on preparing for one of the careers listed in the top twenty. It would certainly be a good bet in terms of future employment prospects and it helps to narrow down the choices.

Registered nurse, which is often mentioned as a field offering superb employment opportunities, is not listed above because a bachelor's degree is not required for an entry-level position, even though it pays as well as many jobs requiring four years of college. A search of openings requiring only two years of post-secondary education will yield some very appealing results, some of which pay more than fields requiring college degrees. This can be a wake-up call for most high school students who have been led to believe that college is the only path to success.

Internet research is a great place to begin assessing the prospects for any career possibility. The best sources of information on specific career fields will always be people working in the industries themselves, however, because they are closest to the action. Any connections you have in fields of interest can prove very valuable in locating helpful career information and advance notice of possible job openings.

The Importance of Networking

When parents or students don't have direct contacts in a field, informational interviewing can be very helpful in uncovering useful insights and making connections. Try contacting influential and well-positioned people and asking for a few moments of their time. You may be surprised at how willing they are to speak with you and share what they know. Come prepared with insightful questions and thank them profusely for their help. Invite them to join your social network, afterward. If you make a good impression, this person might open doors, since forward-thinking individuals are always on the lookout for bright, inquisitive, and capable people. Some people have found wonderful mentors and priceless job contacts in this way.

REALITY RULE #20

OLD RULE:	NEW RULE:
Your college degree will get you a job.	*Your resume, "brand," and personal contacts will get you a job.*

Prior generations could rely on their college degrees to help them land a good job. The mere presence of a newly minted bachelor's degree, proudly displayed at the top of a resume, was enough to impress potential employers, especially when there were plenty of jobs to go around.

Today, getting hired is more difficult. When a potential employer is looking at a huge stack of resumes from applicants, he needs to make tough choices to begin whittling it down to a manageable number. Your resume is going to have to include more than a college degree to attract attention. One of the quickest ways in which many employers will weed through an overwhelming pile of applications is to rely on networks of personal contacts to recommend someone for the job. Remember the old saying, "It's not what you know, but who you know"? Well, this is one of the times when it really applies. It is certainly not fair, and it does not guarantee that the employer will find the best or most qualified applicant in the pool, but in the real world people are often hired based on their connections.

BUILD YOUR NETWORKS!

This is why it is so important to use college as a time to build personal and professional networks in your field of interest. This means making the most of opportunities to meet other students—and their *parents*—in college rather than spending all your time in your dorm room studying. It also means making optimal use of online networking sites and the opportunities they provide to connect with people in your career area. If you cultivate useful contacts, you will find a growing list of reliable friends in your field of endeavor who can introduce you to important people, notify you of upcoming job openings, and recommend you. Of course, you should also maintain good relationships with your faculty members for the same reason, although in my experience many faculty members remain immersed in the academic world and sometimes lose contact with the "outside" employment world. You should definitely try to tap your college professors for help with your job search, but don't be surprised if you have to move beyond them to locate the most helpful contacts.

Today, with the ease of communication offered by social networking, there is no reason why college students can't reach out to well-known, respected individuals and try to establish a personal connection. Another way to meet influential people is by attending professional conferences. Make the investment to join relevant professional organizations in your field. Such organizations hold annual conferences as well as regional meetings. Attend these conferences, and network diligently. Parents who want to help their students find employment should consider picking up the tab for organizational dues and travel to professional conferences. These are the sorts of events where students can meet influential people with the capability to hire them.

Building a Professional Image and Brand

Students who want to be hired need to polish and refine their professional image. You must be clear about where you are heading. There is a saying that the world stands aside to make room for a person who knows where he is going. This is another way of saying that people who know what they want in life usually get it. You want to become coherent and sophisticated in the way that you present yourself so that people remember you and recognize your direction in life.

What can you do better than anyone else? What kind of work can you perform? These are the things you want other people to notice and remember about you and you need to communicate them. This will become part of the personal "brand" that you will use to market yourself. A student with a clear, recognizable brand is likely to receive opportunities ahead of students with vague and unclear aspirations or abilities.

Branding expert and author of *Me 2.0* Dan Schawbel says, "Personal branding is about unearthing what is true and unique about you and letting everyone know about it." Martin Yate, the author of *Knock 'em Dead Resumes,* says that career success is much easier to achieve when you are "credible and visible" within your profession. This means creating a professional brand as part of an overall career management strategy. Yate points out that this takes time, but "you have to start somewhere and you need to start now."

A big part of developing a recognizable brand is having a focused, consistent message. Above all, you need to identify the competitive differences that will set you apart from the other candidates. Of course, this requires a great deal of reflection, maturity, and identity development, which is a big part of what the college years are about.

Branding goes beyond the traditional methods of applying for jobs, which fail for so many applicants. It also takes full advantage of technology by building a searchable, recognizable Internet presence. According to Schawbel, college students should be building and promoting a personal brand online through websites, blogs, and social media. Each of these elements builds on the others to reinforce your image and serve as an online billboard to advertise your talents. In other words, it's not just who you know that is important; it's also important who knows you!

Make Your Brand Personal

Many students rely on the name of their undergraduate college to be their brand. This is certainly part of a branding strategy, but it is not a substitute for a brand of your own. It does make sense for a new entrant to the workforce to associate with a well-established brand name, such as a prestigious college. Your dream employer may not have heard of you, but hopefully he has heard of your school! If the school has a good reputation, then some positive associations will be transferred onto you. This is what Schawbel refers to as "Strategic Brand Association." You leverage the reputation of the well-known brand to enhance your own credibility. This can work reasonably well in some cases, but it does not exempt you from developing and maintaining a personal brand that will serve you throughout your entire career.

Your individual brand consists of:

- **Your reputation**

- **Your image**

- **Your credentials**

- **Your work history**

- **Samples of your work**

- **Your reputation or endorsements**

Also, be sure to collect letters of recommendation—both from professors and employers—throughout your entire college career and from every employer afterward. It is important to think of each professor or boss not merely as the person who will grade or pay you, but also as the person who will recommend you to people offering even bigger opportunities in the future. Make friends with them and do a good job for them.

Grow Your Online Presence

Likewise, you should continue building and refining your online presence throughout college. Of course, you are there to study and learn, but you are also there to meet people and network. This is easily as important as what goes on in the classroom. Beyond campus, identify the people in your desired field whom you most admire, work up your nerve, and send them an e-mail. You might compliment them on a published article or congratulate them on a recent success. Better yet, locate some information they might find useful and share it with them. Don't be offended if you don't hear back, but don't be surprised if you do. Some of them may respond positively and then you can send them an invitation to connect on LinkedIn or Facebook.

Make it a habit to be generous with the people in your growing online networks. By offering assistance to others, you develop allies who will be willing to support and assist you when you begin to search for a position. You should continue to build your brand throughout your college years, remembering that your academic transcript is only one small part of it.

When you are ready to apply for specific career positions, it is time to launch the brand you have been refining throughout college and to activate your network to help you achieve your goals. Reach out to your list of personal contacts to see if anyone knows of an appropriate opening and can help connect you to a decision-maker. Ask for introductions to influential individuals.

It would be nice if colleges and their career centers would help students with personal branding. Unfortunately, this is unlikely to happen on the majority of campuses any time soon. Consider this an opportunity to stand out from the rest of the pack and build an unforgettable personal brand that will enhance your resume and inspire your personal contacts to want to assist you. In terms of increasing your potential to be hired, networking and branding are two extracurricular activities you must not skip.

REALITY RULE #21

OLD RULE:	NEW RULE:
Once the kid graduates, he's on his own financially.	Parents may have to help graduates more now after college, especially with their first job search.

After investing tens or even hundreds of thousands of dollars on a college degree, it is understandable that parents want to sit back and assume that their child's future is set and their work is done. Unfortunately, as the majority of parents are now discovering, this can turn out to be extremely wishful thinking.

According to *www.collegegrad.com*, an alarming 80 percent of recent graduates failed to find a job and 80 percent moved right back in with their parents. The National Association of Colleges and Employers also found that four out of five new graduates had no job offers at graduation. A majority of these graduates still had student loans to repay, despite their unemployed status. Even possessing an elite degree is no guarantee of employment: Harvard's Office of Career Services reported that two out of three recent graduates did not have a job at graduation.

THE "LOST GENERATION"

Parents are understandably anxious about the future prospects for their children and more and more families are finding their adult children landing back in their childhood bedrooms after failing to find self-supporting jobs post-graduation. Many of these parents are rightly afraid that their children are in peril of becoming part of a new, "lost generation." There is no doubt that the job market for young adults in the United States is bleak right now. Reports indicate that only 31 percent of young workers currently earn enough money to cover their bills and that one in three young workers lives at home with their parents.

KIPPERS ABROAD

Think this trend of young people living at home in their twenties, or beyond, is just happening in America? Hardly. In England, they call them *KIPPERS*, which stands for "Kids in Parents' Pockets Eroding Retirement Savings." In Japan, they are *parasite singles*. In Italy, they call the 60 percent of young adults between eighteen and thirty-four who live at home *bamboccioni*, which stands for *big babies*. Whatever you call them, they are young adults living at home with their parents long after prior generations would have moved out. Many of these young adults say they have no choice but to rely upon their parents for help because they cannot find steady jobs that pay enough money to afford homes of their own.

Nearly every family in America knows a young college graduate who is either unemployed or working a subsistence job while seeking career employment with benefits. The government even seems to be preparing families for an era of European style underemployed young people by making arrangements to keep young adults on their parents' health-care plans until age twenty-six. This is not the future most parents want for their children or themselves. Everyone's goal is for graduates to be independent and self-supporting after college. You will need to be proactive, however, to beat the distressing odds.

The fact of the matter is that adolescence in America has grown longer. There are many reasons for this trend. One is our increasing lifespan, which seems to have afforded young people a longer amount of time before they have to grow up and settle down. Demography, however, is another huge factor in this phenomenon. As the older, larger boomer generation postpones retirement, this limits opportunities for younger people to enter and advance in the workforce. This is why it is so important to take steps now to prepare this generation of students to be employable, not just college-educated.

Young People Adrift

We are seeing rising levels of unrest among discontented youth, and it is not surprising, when you examine the dire statistics. It appears that young people worldwide are beginning to catch on to the raw economic hand they have been dealt. In America, we see growing awareness of the unsustainable student loan debts being foisted on the young. Already we have seen college student riots in Italy and England over rising tuition fees and higher education cutbacks. Young people in Greece and France have rioted over reduced job protection and other benefits that were extended to their parents' generation at a cost so large that the only way to finance it is to strip younger people of the same privileges while asking them to pay for it. Large-scale riots in Tunisia and Egypt that resulted in regime change were initially driven by unemployed youth. The "Occupy Wall Street" movement in New York and across America features an undercurrent of anger at the banking system over student loans. This is part of a larger societal problem that is partly demographic in nature and not of their making. So, parents should be empathetic, but also prepared to offer students practical help to beat the odds and to make the transition to full-time employment. Families of college students must plan to be actively involved after commencement to ensure they can gain a foothold in the new economy, which merely underscores the need to preserve a portion of limited family assets for assisting a child post-graduation.

REALITY RULE #22

OLD RULE:	NEW RULE:
Find a safe, secure job and stay in it until retirement.	*Always be prepared to make your own job.*

This book is all about reexamining tired, traditional college advice. Some of this advice is left over from another age when it presumably worked fairly well, but following it today can have disastrous results, as I hope you now understand. This last career-oriented rule is not just for the next generation of college students, but for their parents, as well.

As many of us have learned, the working world is an unpredictable and often unforgiving place. It changes rapidly, often without warning. While our parents (the grandparents of the

current college generation) may have enjoyed lifetime employment with one company and secure pensions, this dream is fall-
ing apart for an increasing number of families. It appears that
we have reached the end of the industrial age, when Americans
were offered the bargain to give up some of their autonomy
to work for large organizations, which, in return, promised to
supply a steady paycheck and income during retirement. This
model is collapsing, and it is not yet clear what will be taking
its place.

No one is sure what will replace the lost manufacturing
jobs that once provided such reliable employment for so many
middle-class Americans. The fear is that these jobs will never
return. Even the public sector, which seemed to be the safest,
most secure portion of the economy, is under pressure.

If a student is lucky enough to find what appears to be
a secure job, that is great, but, as an increasing number of
Americans are learning, even jobs that seemed secure can suddenly be lost without warning. Nothing in life is ever certain.
We all need a smarter way of planning for the future that will
protect us from the fickleness of sudden, unpredictable changes
in the economy and the decreasing loyalties of employers to
employees.

JOB-*PLUS*

The same principle that will help a student to stand apart from
other college graduates—College-*Plus*—can also help to add
extra security and flexibility when applied to careers, and this
is a strategy that anyone, including parents, can use. I think
of it as Job-*Plus*. You must take more personal responsibility

for your career than simply relying on an employer to choose you from a stack of applicants and supply you with a paycheck and list of expected job duties. Instead, acknowledge that your career is always your own responsibility, and you must always be working at it regardless of who is writing the paycheck at the moment. If no one else offers you work, you must sail your own ship and employ yourself.

To succeed in the new economy, workers need to be adaptable, flexible, and in charge of their own fate. As the writer Joseph Campbell once said, "The insecure way is the secure way." Tomorrow's workers are going to find that going to college once, for four years, is not nearly enough education to last for an entire career. Instead, they will have to retrain for new careers as jobs realign and the knowledge base expands more rapidly. A successful worker will read the writing on the wall and recognize when the economy is shifting in a new direction.

Job-*Plus* can mean thinking like an independent contractor, even when employed in a secure job with benefits. It can mean supplementing your existing job with an outside, entrepreneurial endeavor. This way, you always have a backup plan and will never be unemployed or thrown out of work. Strive to identify a need and then find a way to meet it better than anyone else can. That will always be the key to success in any economic climate. A worker's ability to read the signs of change, spot opportunity, think, innovate, and adapt will always be the greatest job security possible.

The Uncertain Future

You never know what's going to happen. The future for today's graduates is very unpredictable. Sudden financial crises can throw people out of work mid-career. While the Internet created many high-paying jobs for those flexible enough to seize the new opportunities, it also wreaked havoc on employment in publishing, advertising, and the news media. Forces such as globalization have changed entire industries and continue to transform the global economy. There is no way of knowing exactly how all these forces will play out, but an informed person can make educated guesses that may pay off.

Fortunately, the free enterprise system remains open for business to all and is always hiring. We have been deluded into thinking that we have to be hired by an employer to earn money, but that is simply not true. That is just the old work formula. Identify problems and offer valuable solutions that work. That's the new formula for success today and that is something people will always be willing to pay for.

Decision-making expert H. B. Gelatt argues that we all have to learn to make career choices even in the face of considerable uncertainty. You want to remove as much of the uncertainty as possible, but you will never eliminate it entirely. You must still make positive decisions for moving forward, in spite of ambiguity, remembering that your direction can be corrected, as necessary. As the song goes, you can't control the wind, but you can adjust your sails. College students must remember, as well, that much of what is learned in college, no matter how carefully chosen, will be outdated very rapidly. Continuous lifelong learning is now necessary, and being cautious about overspending on a bachelor's degree will allow more funds later for updating your knowledge and skill base to match emerging opportunities.

Job security is an illusory concept—one that a college diploma certainly cannot guarantee. It is not just college students who are waking up to the demise of this cherished part of the traditional American Dream. Hundreds of thousands of unemployed, middle-aged adults are facing the same harsh reality. Ultimately, the most successful careers will come from relying on yourself rather than on others or on faceless organi- zations. A person who can make his own job throughout life will always be successfully employed. Whether you are fresh out of college or have been in the workforce for decades, you should always be prepared to take your destiny in your own hands and create your own ideal job.

COLLEGE— AT WHAT COST?

G oing to college today is a very different enterprise than it was in decades past. Today's students face a more competitive admissions environment and a much more difficult time establishing themselves in their first jobs. Topping it all off are steeply higher tuition prices that are placing family finances and future budgets in jeopardy.

To succeed despite the odds, families first need to recognize and acknowledge that all the rules have changed—dramatically. Then, they need to adapt what they are doing to make the most of their postsecondary opportunities within this altered context.

Is college still worth it? It certainly can be . . . but not at any price. Higher education is still a noble endeavor and well worth pursuing, but there is obviously an upper limit to the amount of money that a family can devote to tuition while still expecting a favorable economic return on the investment.

Hopefully, the current higher education affordability crisis will subside and prices will fall to more reasonable levels. I am confident that the same inexorable forces of supply and demand that lowered housing prices will also eventually assert themselves to bring about a much-needed correction to runaway tuition prices. As the saying goes, what can't last . . . won't. This applies to a college bubble as well as to any other type of economic inflation.

I am also confident that inevitable demographic forces will eventually yield a much more welcoming job environment as the baby boomers retire and jobs for America's youth become more plentiful. Meanwhile, I hope that the rules outlined here will help your family to improve your odds of obtaining a reasonably priced degree that provides access to promising and available job opportunities.

I still believe in college the same way I still believe in owning a home. However, I'm also glad I didn't invest in overpriced real estate during the peak of the housing bubble and ruin my family's financial stability. There are times to be confident and take risks when allocating your hard earned money and there are times to be cautious and exercise restraint. Now is a time for self-control in higher education expenditures.

Both generations must work together to overcome the challenges of the current higher education and employment climates. Parents: Use sound financial judgment when deciding how much college you can afford and look out for your student's long-term interests when it comes to assuming debt. Students: Remember that your parents will need to retire someday and that financial considerations need to play a role in your college decisions. Be reasonable in your college choices and proactive in your career preparation. Jobs are not going to come looking for you. You are going to have to make your first job happen. Most importantly, remember that college is what you make of it—not what you pay for it. It always has been, and it always will be.

Good luck!

10 STEPS TO LAUNCHING A COLLEGE STUDENT INTO THE WORKFORCE

1. Every college applicant should already have a resume, including a stated career goal, to submit to the Admissions Office.

2. Every college freshman needs to be familiar with the college career center. Parents and students, when you first arrive on campus, locate the career center and visit it. Students should check in regularly to look for summer employment and seek other advertised opportunities.

3. Students, try to get an on-campus job working in the career center. If you succeed, you will be the first to know when new job openings appear.

4. Don't confuse volunteer community service or unpaid internships with paying jobs. A college graduate should have at least three *paying* jobs listed on his resume. The more professional the jobs, the better.

5. Collect letters of recommendation from professors throughout college. This is also a reminder to stay on good terms with them!

6. Build a career network. This process can begin by shifting your most helpful social networking contacts on Facebook to a more professional location, such as LinkedIn, but should grow to include employers, professors, and others able to provide references.

7. Parents, pay for your offspring to attend relevant professional conferences and meetings during college. This is money very well spent.

8. Parents, work your own professional network on behalf of a student throughout college. Set up informational interviews or job shadowing for your child with appropriate friends. If you don't have your own network, begin building it!

9. Reality check career goals by using resources such as *www.careeronestop.org, www.collegegrad.com*, and *www.salary.com*.

10. Remember that launching students into self-supporting adulthood today requires a family effort. Get involved early and stay involved.

RECOMMENDED RESOURCES

College Selection

www.collegeboard.com
www.collegeprowler.com/
www.ratemyprofessors.com
www.studentsreview.com

Financial Aid

www.fafsa.ed.gov
www.finaid.org
www.planettuition.com

EFC Calculators

www.finaid.org/calculators/finaidestimate.phtml
www.fafsa4caster.ed.gov

Scholarships

www.collegescholarships.org
www.fastweb.com
www.scholarships.com

Merit Aid

www.meritaid.com

College Majors

www.collegeboard.org

www.mymajors.com

Career Planning

www.careerinfonet.org

www.careeronestop.org

www.collegeboard.com/csearch/majors_careers/profiles

www.collegegrad.com

www.onetonline.org

www.people2capital.com (Human capital score™: an unbiased ranking and projection of the economic value of an education.)

www.salary.com

www.humanmetrics.com

Workforce Credentials Information Center

www.careeronestop.org/credentialing/credentialinghome.asp

BIBLIOGRAPHY

AFL-CIO. *Young Workers: A Lost Decade*. (Washington DC: Working America, 2010.)

Anderson, Jessica. "Life after college for many means returning home: Recent grads continue to move back in with Mom and Dad." *The Baltimore Sun*, June 20, 2010.

Andre, Vania. "College tuition sending middle class into unprecedented debt." *www.AllMediaNY.com*, June 13, 2011.

Barone, Michael. "Higher education bubble poised to burst." *The Washington Examiner*, September 3, 2010.

Barrow, Lisa and Rouse, Cecilia Elena. "Does college still pay?" *The Economists' Voice*, 24: 2005.

Berrett, Dan. "Not so need-blind." *Inside Higher Ed*, October 29, 2010.

Bissonnette, Zac. *Debt-Free U: How I Paid for an Outstanding College Education Without Loans, Scholarships, or Mooching Off My Parents*. (New York: Portfolio/Penguin, 2010).

Bissonnette, Zac. "One in five federal student loans go into default." *www.DailyFinance.com*, July 7, 2010.

Callahan, Maureen. "Class dismissed: Why middle income jobs are not coming back." *New York Post*, November 14, 2010.

Carney, John. "Sorry Mr. President, we really don't need 8 million more college graduates." *www.CNBC.com*, October 27, 2010.

Clark, Kim. "How much is that college degree really worth?" *U.S. News & World Report,* October 30, 2008.

Cooper, Jasen. "U.S. financial aid system sucks and is stupid." *University of Colorado Scribe,* October 11, 2010.

Crawford, Matthew. *Shop Class As Soulcraft: An Inquiry into the Value of Work.* (New York: Penguin Press, 2009).

DiMeglio, Francesca. "College: Big investment, paltry return." *BusinessWeek,* June 28, 2010.

Dorning, Mike. "College grads flood labor market with diminished prospects." *www.Bloomberg.com,* May 19, 2010.

Elliott, Larry. "Gordon Brown to warn against global youth unemployment epidemic." *The Guardian,* January 18, 2011.

Harvard Graduate School of Education. *Pathways to Prosperity: Meeting the Challenge of Preparing Young Americans for the 21st Century.* (Cambridge, MA: Harvard University Press, 2011).

Jackson, Derrick. "A crisis of spiraling tuition." *Boston Globe,* August 31, 2010.

Jaschik, Scott. "Clashes of money and values: A survey of admissions directors." *Inside Higher Ed,* September 21, 2011.

Klugerman, Yaffa. "Wealth plays role in college admissions." *www.Braintrack.com,* January 31, 2011.

Kristof, Kathy. "The great college hoax." *Forbes,* February 2, 2009.

Levine, Art. "The new 'lost generation': Young workers." *In These Times,* April 9, 2010.

Lieber, Ron. "Placing the blame as students are buried in debt." *New York Times,* May 28, 2010.

Loonin, Deanne. *Paying the Price: The High Cost of Private Student Loans and the Dangers for Student Borrowers.* (Boston, MA: National Consumer Law Center, 2008).

Lore, Nicholas. *Now What? The Young Person's Guide to Choosing the Perfect Career.* (New York: Simon & Schuster, 2008).

Luzer, Daniel. "The prestige racket." *Washington Monthly,* August 23, 2010.

Mannes, George. "Young doctors in debt." *CNN Money,* November 16, 2007.

Morello, Carol. "More college-educated jump tracks to become skilled manual laborers." *The Washington Post,* June 15, 2010.

Moses, Jennifer. "The escalating arms race for top colleges." *The Wall Street Journal,* February 5, 2011.

Naked Law blog. "8 reasons college tuition is the next bubble to burst." *www.Avvo.com,* June 8, 2010.

Olson, Dan. "College debt: A state of 'indentured servitude.'" *The Huffington Post,* February 22, 2010.

Percy, Rosita. "Recurring nightmare of unpaid internships." *The Guardian* Careers Blog, July 29, 2011.

Pilon, Mary. "What's a degree really worth?" *The Wall Street Journal,* February 2, 2010.

Pugh, Tony. "Recession's toll: Most recent college grads working low-skill jobs." *www.McClatchydc.com,* June 25, 2009.

Reynolds, Glenn. "Higher education bubble." *Instapundit,* February 13, 2011.

Reynolds, Glenn. "Higher education's bubble is about to burst." *Washington Examiner,* February 6, 2010.

Sahadi, Jeanne. "College in 4 years? Try 5 or 6." *www. CNNMoney.com,* June 22, 2004.

Schaeffer, Matthew. "Back to the future with Peter Thiel." *National Review Online,* January 20, 2011.

"The coming student loan debacle." *The Weekly Standard,* July 12, 2010.

Uchitelle, Louis. "American dream elusive for millennials." *New York Times,* July 6, 2010.

"Unemployment benefits: The 99ers." CBS *60 Minutes,* October 24, 2010.

Vedder, Richard. "Why did 17 million students go to college?" *The Chronicle of Higher Education,* October 20, 2010.

Warren, Elizabeth. "America without a middle class." *The Huffington Post,* December 3, 2009.

Weston, Liz. "Is your degree worth $1 million—or worthless?" *www.MSNMoney.com,* November 7, 2010.

Wilner, Richard. "The dead end kids: Young, unemployed and facing a tough future." *The New York Post,* September 29, 2009.

Yate, Martin. *Knock 'em Dead Resumes: Standout Advice from America's Leading Job Search Authority.* (Avon, MA: Adams Media, 2010).

INDEX

ABOUT THE AUTHOR

Dr. Bonnie Snyder is a private college/career consultant and Certified College Planning Specialist (CCPS) with the National Institute of Certified College Planners. She is an Honors graduate of Harvard University with a Master's in Counseling and a Doctorate degree in Higher Education. She has served as a high school teacher, guidance counselor, college admissions officer, college professor, and college career counselor. In addition, she is a Global Career Development Facilitator (GCDF) with the National Career Development Association.

Dr. Snyder is also a busy writer and speaker and maintains a blog on college planning at *www.kerrigancollegeplanning.com*. Her Twitter feed is @collegestrategy.